MODERN
UPHOLSTERY

MODERN UPHOLSTERY

BY

DOROTHY COX

LONDON
G. BELL AND SONS, LTD

A Bell Handbook

ISBN 0 7135 1599 6
PRINTED IN GREAT BRITAIN BY
THE CAMELOT PRESS LTD., LONDON AND SOUTHAMPTON

Contents

Acknowledgements

I would like to express my thanks to the many people who by giving so generously of their time and advice have made the preparation of this book possible:

Mrs. Mabel Siddle for so willingly undertaking the typing.

Mrs. Denise Cox for her trouble in travelling to see the pieces of work and her illustrations of them.

Mr. and Mrs. A. H. Parfitt for the time and care they gave when taking the photographs.

Mr. J. C. Adams for his advice and assistance in restoring the frames of some chairs.

The many students who gave their support and encouragement, and particularly those who loaned their work for the photographs.

Dunlop Co. Ltd. and the British-Vita Company for allowing me to visit their factories and giving so generously of their time.

The National Rubber Producers Research Association for their co-operation, and enabling me to make contacts with numerous firms.

My family and colleagues for their tolerance and practical help in checking the script and their general encouragement.

★ 1 ★

The Development of a New Craft

INTEREST IN THE possession of a beautiful home has never been more apparent than it is today. This active interest exists throughout society, aroused and stimulated by magazines, by television, and by the extensive range of fabrics and furniture to be seen in the shops.

Resulting from this interest, many people have acquired a new hobby: namely, searching for, and collecting antiques. To find a beautiful chair frame will bring a tremendous sense of satisfaction, but the ability to renovate it oneself will not only emphasize the pleasure of acquisition, but at the same time will give a sense of achievement.

Apart from re-upholstering attractive 'finds', home upholstery is of great value in repairing and maintaining furniture already in the home. The ability to carry out these repairs, with a professional standard of finish, is an invaluable asset, especially today when labour is so expensive, and in many cases difficult to find. People not interested in old furniture can find that the craft has much to offer them. It is possible to buy new frames, modern in design, which, after being upholstered, will compare favourably with any contemporary furniture.

Upholstery is one of the oldest crafts in civilization. Cushions were man's earliest means of obtaining comfort as he sat or reclined on his hard chair or bench. Gradually the cushions were modified and attached to the pieces of furniture—this was the beginning of upholstery.

Hair, flock, coir fibre and wood wool, are some of the materials used as fillings in Traditional Upholstery, and they

7

are held in position by hessian and scrim.   Good edges are obtained by stitching with upholstery twine.   The control of the fillings and building up of shape requires considerable experience and skill, acquired by few amateurs.

The difficult techniques, together with a shortage of able and willing teachers, prevented this craft achieving a wide popularity in the home, in schools or in centres of further education.

The invention and development of new upholstery materials have completely changed this situation.   Upholstery can now be easily, and what is of even greater importance, successfully, practised by the so-called amateur or 'do-it-yourself' worker.   No craft is more rewarding either aesthetically or financially.   During the last ten years its popularity has become very obvious, as more people recognize the potentialities offered by this craft.

Latex foam was first manufactured in 1929 and a new industry was born.   The manufacture of this material was developed through the 1930's, but it was not until the post-war years that it began to play its present major role in the furniture and allied industries.

The early foam was manufactured from the natural latex of the rubber tree.   Today this natural foam is supplemented by vast quantities of synthetic rubber.   The synthetic rubbers or polyurethanes are of chemical origin.   Of the polyurethanes, polyether foam is the type widely used in the upholstery industry.   Manufacturers are now producing foams in which the two types of foam, natural and synthetic, are blended together.   Certainly latex foam can still be regarded as the Rolls-Royce of Foams, but the price of natural Latex is presenting an ever increasing problem.

LATEX FOAM

Manufacture.   The underlying principle of the manufacture of the foam is that millions of tiny bubbles of air are entrapped in the latex while it is in a semi-liquid state.   Soap is introduced into the liquid latex and the mixture is beaten to form a foam. The length of the beating process determines the quantity of air which is introduced, and hence the final density of the foam. An alternative way of expressing this is that the amount of latex used to fill a given volume will determine the final density of the foam. After the foaming process, a gelling agent, sulphur and anti-oxidants are added. The foam is then fed through a hose to fill various moulds, or to be laid in a thin layer on a continuously moving belt. It is then passed through a heated chamber where it sets. At the same time the sulphur which is present effects the vulcanizing or curing and the foam assumes its familiar resilient form. After this the foam is removed from the moulds, thoroughly washed to remove all the processing chemicals, and finally dried.

During the last four years the manufacturing process has undergone radical changes, and there has been a strong swing to this new method which produces foam known as pin-core foam. The foam is compounded in the continuous mixing head, but no gelling agent is added. It is only partially foamed to produce a high density foam containing minute air bubbles. A measured amount is then piped into the mould which is only partly filled. The mould is then sealed and a vacuum applied. This extracts the air left in the mould and under the reduced pressure the foam expands to fill the mould. The setting or coagulation is achieved by rapidly dropping the temperature and passing carbon dioxide through the foam to act as a permanent setting agent. The foam is then vulcanized by raising the temperature. After being removed from the mould the foam is washed and dried. Foam manufactured by this process has a very even texture apart from the other advantages described on page 13.

POLYURETHANES

The production of these foams, often referred to as synthetic rubber, has increased at a tremendous rate during recent years. They are manufactured by many firms and there is a wide range of these foams on the market. One firm produces at least sixteen different grades of foam, each for a specific purpose and varying in density and degree of hardness. Polyether foam is easily distinguished from latex foam both visually and by touch.

At one time it was inferred that this type of foam was inferior in its properties. Sometimes in order to make economies, low density foam made firm by additives, was used for unsuitable purposes. This resulted in the production of unsatisfactory articles. The initial appearance was attractive but the life of the furniture was very limited.

Polyether foam has undoubtedly a major roll to play in the upholstery industry of the future. Being a man-made product its price is more stable and its availability more predictable than a natural product. Polyether foam can be used with every confidence providing the grade used is suitable for the weight and usage it has to withstand.

TYPES OF LATEX FOAM

Latex foam is available in sheet form or in moulded units.

Plain Sheeting (Diagram 1a). This is available in sheets of approximately 6' × 4' 6" and ½" or 1" in thickness. It is of particular use when upholstering 'drop-in' or 'pincushion' type seats. Plain sheeting has the maximum amount of rubber for any given depth of foam. It is useful for doming where a firm rounded seat is needed. Plain sheeting is also used to upholster the arms of small chairs as in the chair in Plate 12.

Cavity Sheetings (Diagram 1b). Again sheets of this foam are available in sizes of approximately 6' 6" × 5'. Thickness varies from 1" to 4". This type of foam was developed to give the thickest sheet possible, using the smallest amount of

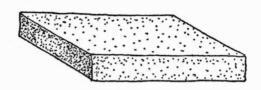

1a. Plain sheet

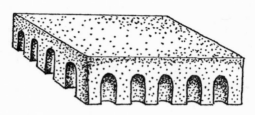

1b. Cavity sheet

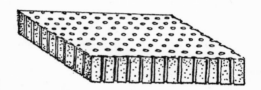

1c. Pin-core sheet

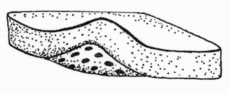

1d. Non-reversible
moulded unit

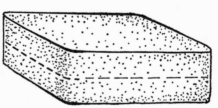

1e. Reversible unit

Diagram 1. Types of Latex Foam

foam. Originally the cavities were rectangular but these have been superseded by circular cavities of smaller diameter. This foam sheet has a smooth skin on one surface, with the cavities visible from the other side. Foam with a very thin skin and large cavities will not produce upholstery which will maintain its shape and stability for a long period. Cavity foam needs walling if a square edge is required. (See Type of Edge—Diagram 16b, page 37.)

Pin-core Foam (Diagram 1c). In this type of foam the cavities have been reduced to approximately $\frac{1}{4}''$ diameter and they pass right through the foam. Pin-core foam has many advantages:

(*a*) Cushions made from pin-core foam are always reversible —even if made from a single sheet of foam.

(*b*) When using pin-core foam for upholstery with a square edge or for making cushions, walling is not necessary as the texture is uniform throughout the sheet.

(*c*) As the cavities are so small there is less risk of the foam being torn in transit, or when being used. There is also less risk of breakdown, during subsequent use of the furniture.

N.B. When pin-core foam has been used for the upholstery, it is necessary to use an undercover of calico over a thin layer of wadding or $\frac{1}{8}''$ polyether foam. If these undercovers are not attached, shadows of the holes in the foam become visible through the covering fabric after the furniture has been used for a short time.

Moulded Units (Diagrams 1d and 1e). These are available in certain sizes and shapes. They have solid walls which are continuous with the top skin, and so further walling is unnecessary. If these are made from a single layer of cavity foam, they are non-reversible. Reversible units are made by joining two non-reversible units with the cavity sides together.

ADVANTAGES OF FOAM IN UPHOLSTERY

Ease of Use. From the upholsterer's point of view the greatest advantage is the ease with which the material can be used. One single process may replace two or three highly skilled techniques of the traditional methods used in this craft.

Cleanliness. It is only when stripping old furniture that this factor is fully appreciated! The foam itself does not break down, nor does it collect dust as the more traditional fillings are inclined to do. Furthermore, it is immune to attack by insects or mildew.

Hygienic Properties. The latex foam itself is completely free from attack by bacteria. Polyether foam is given germicidal properties by additives. The hygienic properties of foam are illustrated by the extent to which it is used in hospitals.

Comfort. As these foams are very resilient, furniture upholstered with foam gives a high degree of comfort. This is closely connected with the density and hardness of the foam. (See Buying Foam, below.)

Cost. Although at first sight the cost may not appear to be low, the final cost of the work will be found to be much less than if it has been done through the trade. This, of course, is due to the present high cost of labour, a factor not usually assessed with 'do-it-yourself' work.

BUYING FOAM

Most retailers are willing to supply this in cut square or rectangular shapes. It is important to choose foam of suitable density and hardness—two different properties not to be confused. They determine the comfort and the recovery property. The density depends on the amount of foam present and hence affects the price of the foam. Hardness of Polyether foam is affected by additives—the foam must not be so soft that the base can be felt. This should always be tested before buying. The resilience of Latex foam is immediate:

with Polyether foam the recovery may be slower, but none the less complete.

The foam chosen must be suitable for the task it has to do, i.e. for the weight it has to support and the hardness of wear it has to withstand. It is important that neither hardness nor the shape of the work shall deteriorate after a short period of use, and so the old adage applies when buying foam —'The best pays in the end'.

Ageing of Foam. The condition which will cause deterioration of the foam is exposure to light for prolonged periods. This is more evident with Latex foam than Polyurethane foam. After prolonged exposure the surfaces of either type of foam will discolour, and eventually begin to crumble. The average upholstery cover is sufficient in itself to exclude the light, although in most upholstery an underlayer of calico is used, so avoiding any risk of damage by light penetrating the cover. Whenever removable covers are being fitted, as on cushions, an undercover should be used.

CLEANING LATEX FOAM UPHOLSTERY

If possible, covers should not be allowed to become too soiled. Frequent dusting with the vacuum cleaner removes loose dust. More persistent dirt may possibly be removed by sponging with a soapy cloth and then wiping with a clean cloth. Always test on a piece of spare material or on the bottom of the back of the chair if cleaning instructions have not been given when the material was bought.

In the last few years aerosol upholstery cleaners have been developed, and are extremely effective. They can be used on fabrics when it is impossible to sponge them with water. These cleaners are sprayed on to the surface of the cover and they do not penetrate to the foam. After drying, the furniture is brushed with a soft clean brush. Petrol, and similar solvent-based cleaners should not be used on covers which cannot be removed, as they damage the foam. Plastic coated fabrics can be wiped over with warm soapy water.

Leather should be kept supple by regular treatment with polish.

Foam upholstery is a craft with tremendous possibilities. It can be used to create new articles or to restore the old. The speed with which work of high quality, and comparatively low cost, can be completed, makes it a craft which will appeal to a wide range of craftsmen and women.

★ 2 ★

Tools and Materials

ONE OF THE attractive aspects of this craft is that most of the tools required will be found in almost every household. In fact anyone making their first stool could probably manage without buying any additional tools. As enthusiasm grows and more ambitious work is attempted, then an upholstery hammer will be found more satisfactory than an ordinary small-headed household hammer and a stripping chisel more satisfactory than an old screwdriver for removing tacks.

SUGGESTED TOOLS (Diagram 2)

Cabriole Hammer. This will have a strong shaft and a small end to the head. The small head enables tacks to be hammered into restricted spaces. It also decreases the risk of damaging any polished parts of the furniture. One end may be very small and possibly magnetic for picking up the tacks. The other end is larger in diameter for driving home the tacks. Other upholstery hammers have one end approximately $\frac{5}{8}''$ diameter with the opposite end shaped as a claw for removing tacks.

Stripping Chisel. This should have a sharp end so that it may be driven under the heads of tacks which have to be removed. (See Method of Stripping—Diagram 8.)

Tack Lifter. This an optional extra, and it provides an additional means of removing tacks. It is particularly useful when leverage is necessary.

Pincers or Pliers. These are used for holding short lengths of webbing which require stretching.

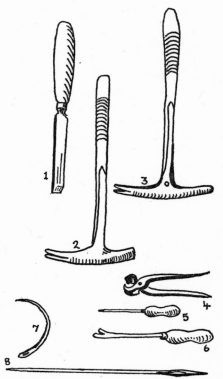

Diagram 2. Tools used in Upholstery

1. Stripping chisel.
2. Cabriole hammer with $\frac{5}{8}''$ head and claw.
3. Cabriole hammer with $\frac{3}{8}''$ head and claw.
4. Pincers. 5. Bradawl.
6. Tack lifter. 7. Half-circular needle.
8. Mattress needle

Scissors. It is an advantage to have both kitchen and dress-making scissors. The former with serrated edges cut easily through the foam; the latter are used for cutting the various fabrics used. A sharp carving knife is useful for cutting through the thicker polyether foam.

Mattress Needles. These are long needles used for buttoning. These needles are obtainable in various lengths but a 10″ or 12″ needle is recommended. They are pointed at both ends with a hole at one end. These needles should be handled with care and stored with a cork on each end.

Half Circular Needles. These are obtainable in various sizes and are used when it is difficult to stitch with an ordinary straight sewing needle. (See Diagram 50.)

Brace and Bit. The bit should be approximately $\frac{1}{2}''$. These are used to bore the ventilation holes when a solid base is being used. Plywood or blockboard may splinter when the holes are being bored. This is prevented by boring the holes until the end of the bit just penetrates the wood. The base is then turned over and the bit inserted in each small hole and the boring completed. The holes will then be cleanly cut on both surfaces of the base. An $\frac{1}{8}''$ or $\frac{3}{16}''$ bit is used when making holes through board for buttoning.

Felt Pen. This is used for marking the foam. It makes the mark smoothly and easily without biting into the foam or causing any tearing.

Round-ended Knife. For spreading on the adhesive.

Yardstick or Long Rule.

Sewing Equipment. In addition, normal sewing equipment such as assorted needles, dressmaking pins, tape measure etc. will be used as the need arises.

MATERIALS

Webbing. Traditional webbing may be used as a base for foam upholstery but many workers find the newer rubberized Pirelli webbing much easier to use, and it has a very long life. This webbing is made with a central layer of rubber between two layers of corded material cut on the bias. It is extremely strong and can be used to replace springs when re-upholstering old furniture. Pirelli webbing is used stretched or tensioned to give a firm but elastic seat. It decreases the probability of the seat losing its shape through the stretching or breaking of the webbing foundation. Pirelli webbing is made in several widths but the $1\frac{1}{2}''$ and $2''$ widths will be found adequate for all needs arising in home upholstery. The method of application is described in the next chapter.

Calico.   Unbleached calico is used for the strips which attach
the foam to the wooden base or frame, and for an undercover when this is necessary.   The strips of calico used for
attaching the foam should always be torn and not cut.
Tearing leaves a fluffy edge which moulds into the foam.
Cutting produces a hard edge which may show through the
top cover, collecting dirt and eventually wearing through the
top material.

Adhesives.   There are a variety of suitable adhesives on the
market.   They should produce joints which are soft and
pliable after the adhesive has set.   Some adhesives which
can be used include:

> D.S.P.   L107 upholstery solution—Dunlop—obtainable
>   in tubes, 1 pt., 1 qt., and 1-gall. tins.
> Bostik D or 199
> Holdtite upholstery solution 9A or 27
> Phillisol rubber cement
> Bateman's non-flam rubber solution

In 1968 a new aerosol adhesive—Scotch Grip—came on to
the market.   This is particularly useful with polyether foam.
It can be sprayed on to the foam, calico, or wood, and produces a very flexible join.   The two surfaces are both sprayed
and should be left about thirty seconds before they are
placed one on the other.   It is only produced in one size for
domestic use and one tin covers approximately 100 sq. ft.
After use the container should be inverted and the button
pressed.   This will blow the system clear of adhesive and
avoid the nozzle becoming blocked.   When joining two
treated surfaces the maximum pressure should be applied.
There is no danger that the foam will remain compressed.

Wadding.   This is used over pin-core foam.   It is placed
beneath the calico under-cover to avoid the cavities of pin-
core foam showing through the first cover.   It is also used—
possibly folded to one or four thicknesses—to pad the edge of
a wooden frame when the covering is being taken over the

19

frame. It may be bought from haberdashery departments and from upholstery shops.

French Chalk or Talcum Powder. Effectively removes any excess adhesive. French chalk is best sprinkled out of a pepper-pot.

Tacks. Upholsterer's tacks and not tacks from a hardware store are essential. They are designed so that they are extremely sharp and will easily pierce the wooden frame or base. It should be rarely necessary to hold a tack while it is hammered into position.

(a) *Improved Tacks.* Have large heads. $\frac{5}{8}''$ or $\frac{1}{2}''$ improved tacks are used for attaching webbing—the large head sitting on top of the webbing.

(b) $\frac{1}{2}''$ *Clout Nails.* Can be used on more delicate woodwork to attach Pirelli webbing.

(c) *Fine Tacks.* These are used for the main upholstery: $\frac{3}{8}''$ are most commonly used but $\frac{1}{2}''$ fine can be used where material is thick or bulky.

(d) *Gimp Pins.* Are used for attaching gimp or braid trimmings, or where an ordinary tack would be unsightly. They are obtainable in a wide range of colours to match the various trimmings and materials.

(e) *Studs and Nails.* These are used as an alternative method of neatening the edges of upholstery, usually on heavier furniture or that which is leather covered. To insert them successfully requires considerable care. They are prone to get out of line and this spoils the finished appearance. They are placed so that they are touching and so completely cover the edge of the covering material. The most successful way of inserting them is to make a

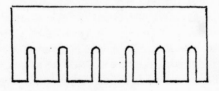

Diagram 3. Template for inserting studs

template (Diagram 3) and mark the position of each stud or nail before any are inserted. Preliminary boring with a bradawl helps to ensure that the nail enters the wood at the correct angle. When driving them into position the top of the nail should be protected by a piece of soft material or felt.

COVERING MATERIALS

There is a very large range of materials suitable for covering furniture. The range has recently been widened still further by the production of many furnishing fabrics using man-made fibres. Many of these fabrics have the additional property that they are stain resistant and may be successfully sponged over with water. Dralon velvet has become very popular for this reason, and other new fabrics include Acrilan fur-fabric; materials which are mixtures of natural and man-made fibre; also P.V.C. coated fabrics, and stretch fabrics.

In addition to the materials made from the new fibres the more traditional upholstery materials, including moquettes, velvets, tapesteries, brocades, and tweeds, can all be used successfully. The important factor is that the material chosen shall be suitable for the amount of wear and strain which will be demanded of it.

A general rule is that the covering fabric should be closely woven. Open-weave fabrics are much more prone to wear quickly as the friction produced by the threads moving causes them to fray and break. Open-weave fabrics also allow light to penetrate to the foam and deterioration will occur.

Worked Canvases. Many embroideresses prefer to work the covers for chairs and this can produce difficulties when it is necessary to slash the cover. These difficulties can be overcome by using a woven iron-on interlining, such as Staflex. This should be attached to the underside of the canvas wherever it needs to be slashed. This method can also be used if old canvases are to be removed and then re-used. In this case a piece of Staflex 2″–3″ larger than the canvas, can be ironed to the wrong side of the whole canvas. This will strengthen any parts weakened by age and also give a border, making handling easier.

Linings. Hessian, black linen, or upholsterer's lining are used to neaten the underneath of chair seats.

TRIMMINGS

Piping. There is now on the market nylon cord which is much to be preferred to the older cotton cord. This cord will not shrink when washed, so it is not necessary to boil it before use. As it has a smooth surface it is less liable to wear through the covering of the piping. Two types of this nylon cord are available, one having a much harder texture—this should only be used with heavier materials. The softer cord, which has a 'silky' texture, should be used with lighter weight fabrics. This cord is more frequently found in hardware stores than the usual haberdashery departments of large furnishing stores. There are two ways of making crossway covering. When a comparatively short length is required to go round a small stool, separate lengths can be cut and these joined together as shown in Diagrams 4a, 4b, 4c below.

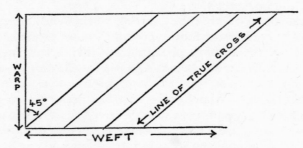

Diagram 4a. Cutting short crossway strips

If a large amount of piping is needed, it is much quicker to make a 'sleeve' by the following method.

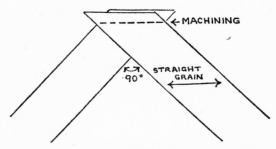

Diagram 4b. Method of joining crossway strips

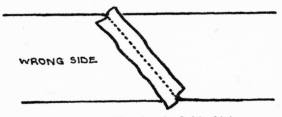

Diagram 4c. Showing the finished join

1. Take a rectangle of fabric—at least 9″ wide—and fold up the lower right-hand corner, bringing C up to the top edge AB and crease well (Diagrams 5a and 5b).

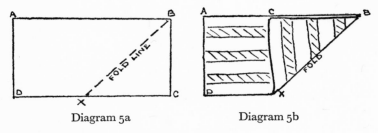

Diagram 5a   Diagram 5b

2. Cut off this corner along line BX.
3. Transfer triangle BXC to the opposite end of the rectangle (Diagram 5c).

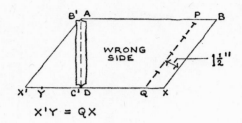

X'Y = QX

Diagram 5c

4. Fold the triangle over on to the remaining material right sides together, baste, and machine with a very SMALL STITCH. Press the seam open: a parallelogram will have been formed.
5. On the wrong side mark line PQ $1\frac{1}{4}''$–$1\frac{1}{2}''$ from BX (Diagram 5c).
6. Fold as shown in Diagram 5d below, baste the long edges A–P and X–Y together—PB remains free. Machine with a SMALL stitch. A tube with the seam running spirally will be formed. This is known as a sleeve (Diagram 5d).

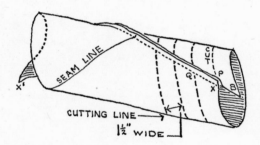

Diagram 5d

7. Cut along the dotted line from P to Q and continue cutting until the whole sleeve has been used—keeping the strip a uniform width.

Whichever method is used for making the piping strip, it should be machine tacked over the cord using a piping or zipper foot. This will act as a barrier line when it is necessary to slash the piping when going around corners (Diagram 6).

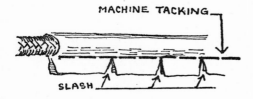

Diagram 6

The final join of the ends of crossway strips should be *in*distinguishable from other joins. Each end of the piping cord should be thinned to half its thickness for the last inch. The method of doing this varies according to the structure of the cord. The two thinned ends should overlap for the inch and be bound together (Diagrams 7a and 7b).

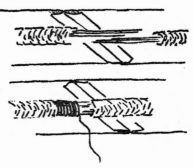

Diagram 7a and b. Joining nylon piping cord

Trimmings. These are used to neaten the edge of the covering materials. Scroll gimps and flat braids are used with woven fabric covers, and bandings with leather or P.V.C. materials.

Twine. This is used when buttoning upholstery. It is a very strong thread obtainable from upholstery shops.

N.B. When 'tacking' with a needle and cotton is required the word 'baste' has been used to avoid confusion with 'hammer and tacks'.

★ 3 ★

Preparing the Frame or Base

THE STRIPPING AND preparation of the frame is possibly the most time-consuming part of repairing a piece of furniture, yet it is of the greatest importance. It is only when the old upholstery is being removed that one realizes and appreciates the extent to which cleanliness and hygiene are two of the great virtues of this new type of upholstery. Dust of years has collected between the fibres of hair or coir fibre, and it is impossible for this to be removed by normal cleaning.

N.B. As the wood of the frame has lost all the natural oils during its years in a heated room, great care must be taken in order not to split the wood when removing the old tacks. Stripping is most easily accomplished with the aid of a stripping chisel and mallet, or hammer. Instructions usually suggest using a mallet, but a hammer can be equally successful if it is used as in Diagram 8 below.

The hammer is turned and used so that the side of the head comes in contact with the head of the chisel. This avoids sore knuckles caused by the head of the hammer missing the chisel. The end of the chisel is placed under the head of the tack or just in front of it and angled so that it will be driven under the tack. The handle of the chisel is then firmly hit with the centre of the side of the hammer.

It is most IMPORTANT when stripping in this manner to work *with the grain of the wood*. If the chisel is hammered at right angles to the grain it is very easy to knock out a section of wood or to split the frame.

The same method is used to remove any tacks incorrectly inserted during re-upholstery. A tack lifter or pincers can be used to supplement the above method, but they are insufficient on their own.

Diagram 8. Method of stripping old upholstery

Once the stripping is completed the frame must be cleaned and examined for cracks or woodworm. If necessary it should be treated with 'Rentokil' or 'Cuprinol' and the tack holes filled with plastic wood.

The finish of the polished wood should also be examined. This may have become very dark, almost black, due firstly to many applications of polish, and secondly to the collection of dirt and grime, and the beauty of the wood may have been completely lost. With valuable antique furniture it is wise to seek the advice of an expert before cleaning the wood. However, with care and patience it is possible to improve the appearance of most wooden frames and to restore the beauty of the natural graining of the wood.

Accumulated wax can be removed by using a scraper—the blade of a penknife, or the edge of a penny. This is held at 90° and drawn backwards and forwards over the surface of the wood. Care must be taken not to lift the grain or scar the wood. Scraping is followed by rubbing down with fine glass-paper or ooo steel wool. The surface can be continually wiped clean with methylated spirits. The secret of this process is not to rush it. Stripping, cleaning and preparing the frame frequently takes longer than the actual re-upholstery.

When the stripping, cleaning, and rewaxing is completed, then the re-upholstery may be commenced. The first process is to prepare the base on which the upholstery can be built up: i.e. the frame must be webbed.

The reason for the advancement of upholstery as a home-craft is twofold. First, there has been the invention of foam, and secondly, there has been the invention of rubberized webbing. Traditional webbing may be used under Latex Foam but it is more difficult to attach successfully and it has a very much more limited life.

The 1½″ webbing is suitable for small seats and backs of chairs, and the 2″ webbing is ideal for larger seats, but the two widths can be interchanged. If 1½″ webbing only is available for a fairly large seat, then obviously extra webs would be used. Since the webbing is rubberized, it is elastic, and can be used to replace springs, thus eliminating a very demanding process of traditional upholstery. As the webbing extends when weight is placed upon it, the most comfortable seat is obtained by stretching the webbing from 10 to 12½ per cent. It will still 'give' when sat on and give a resilient seat. If the webbing is over-stretched, the seat will be hard and ungiving. If it is under-stretched, the seat will be too soft and the edge of the frame will cut into the thighs. A safe rule is: 'The larger the seat, the more the rubber webbing is stretched.'

When using woven webbing the end is turned in. This is not necessary with rubberized webbing as it does not fray. It is secured by ⅝″ improved tacks or ½″ clout nails. On very delicate furniture ½″ improved tacks may be used. The large heads of these tacks sit on the webbing and do not sink into it.

The cut at the beginning of the webbing should be sloping if possible. The edges of the frame should always be rubbed down with glass-paper before webbing is attached.

Basic Method of Attaching Pirelli Webbing to Wooden Frames

1. Slope the cut edge of the webbing. Place $\frac{1}{4}''$–$\frac{1}{2}''$ from the edge of the frame and secure with three $\frac{5}{8}''$ improved tacks.
2. Lay the webbing across the frame and mark where it reaches the opposite edge. Measure and mark back one-tenth of this length.
3. Stretch the webbing so that the second mark now reaches the edge of the frame. Secure with three tacks, and cut off the webbing. The cut end should be $\frac{1}{4}''$ from the edge of the frame and also from the tacks (Diagrams 9a & b).

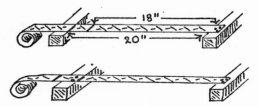

Diagrams 9a and b

N.B. (*a*) The tacks must be driven in at right angles to the webbing and the heads of the tacks sit flat on the webbing. Tacks driven in obliquely will cut the webbing (Diagram 10).

Diagram 10   TACK VERTICAL   TACK AT AN ANGLE

(*b*) It is wasteful to cut off lengths of webbing—it should be applied directly from the roll.

(*c*) If foam is to be applied directly over the webbing it is advisable to web in both directions, weaving in the cross webs. The foam is then protected from the rigid edge of the frame. If the foam is encased in a cover as

29

when a cot mattress or cushion is used over Pirelli webbing, it is adequate to web in one direction only: parallel to the shorter side. The webbing should be more concentrated where the maximum load is likely to occur (Diagrams 11a, 11b and 13).

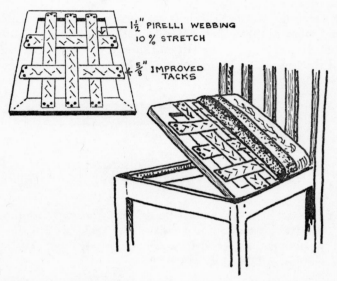

Diagrams 11a and b. The latter showing drop-in seat fully webbed

(*d*) For the most satisfactory results the space between the webs should not exceed the width of the webbing.

(*e*) It is not necessary with rubberized webbing to cover it with hessian as when using traditional webbing. The hessian, being non-elastic, will counteract the advantages of using a rubberized webbing. If traditional webbing is used then hessian must be attached as the strands of rigid webbing would cut into the foam.

(*f*) When two edges of the frame are curved the webbing is only stretched in a direction parallel to the straight edges. Cross webs are still used to protect the foam from the edges of the frame, but they are left unstretched. Examples of this are seen in Chapters 9 & 11 and Diagrams 12 and 64.

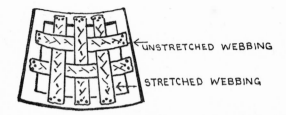

Diagram 12. Webbing a curved frame

Diagram 13. Fireside chair (cross webbing of the back incomplete)

CHAIRS WITH BACK FRAME OF METAL

In some Victorian chairs the frame of the back of the chair is made of metal. There is an outline of tubular or flat strips of metal with further metal strips running horizontally and vertically. It is obviously impossible to tack calico to this frame. Each strip of metal is bound, first with Linter-felt or Upholsterers' wadding and then with strips of calico $1\frac{1}{2}''-2''$ wide. This binding must be done very tightly so that it does not slip when the foam is attached. The calico strips on the foam, the undercover and the outer cover are then all stitched to the back of the bound frame with a strong thread. It is essential to bind all the frame to prevent the metal cutting into the foam.

SOLID BASES

If a chair has a solid base or a stool is being built up on a solid base, 'ventilation holes' must be bored in this base.

The foam contains a considerable volume of air and some of this air is expelled when the seat is used. The expelled air must be able to escape, likewise air must be able to re-enter the foam easily when the pressure is removed—hence the ventilation holes. The holes should be drilled $\frac{1}{2}''$ in diameter and $3''-4''$ apart.

1. Collection of Stools. *Mrs. Bradley, Mrs. Sterland, Author*

2A. Kidney Dressing Stool. *Author*

2B. Pouffe (adapted to fit zebra-hide cover). *Mrs. Hislop*

3. Dining Chairs with drop-in seats. *Author*

4. Stool with drop-in seat. *Mrs. Sterland*

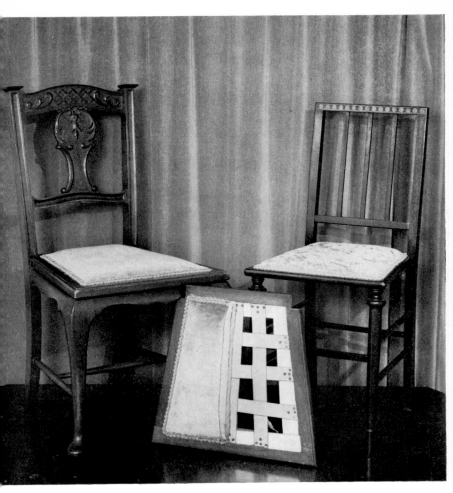

5. Chairs with pincushion seats. *Mrs. Sterland and Author*

6. Upholstered-over Chairs: (a) square edge, (b) rounded edge. *Mrs. Mitchell and Author*

7. Hall Chair (removable upholstered-over seat and drop-in back panel). *Author*

8. Bathroom Chair (back and seat previously caned). *Author*

9. Converted Bentwood Chairs: (a) buttoned back, (b) alternative type of bentwood chair.   *Mrs. O. Cox and Author*

10. Boudoir Chair. *Author*

11A. Victorian buttoned
Chair. *Mrs. King*

11B. Victorian buttoned Chair.
Mrs. Lawton

12. Victorian occasional Chair. *Author*

13. Knitting Chair. *Mrs. Elliott*

14. Cushions for garden furniture. *Author*

15. Bed Head (with drop-in panel) and Chair (loose cushion). *Author*

16. Buttoned Bed Head. *Author*

★ 4 ★

Treatment of Edges of Foam

ONE OF THE most skilled processes in traditional upholstery is the building up of an edge which will withstand the pressure and wear exerted on this part of any seat. Once the edge of upholstery loses its clean line, the furniture becomes shabby in appearance and uncomfortable in use. One of the advantages of foam upholstery is the comparative ease with which a well-shaped and durable edge is achieved.

There are three main ways of treating the edges of foam, and the method chosen determines the ultimate appearance of the upholstery.

FEATHERED EDGE (Diagrams 14a–e)

This type of edge gives a gently rounded edge, suitable for small stools, chairs and drop-in seats. When a feathered edge is being used the foam is cut $\frac{1}{2}''$ larger all round than the base. With cavity or pin-core foam the sides are tapered back at an angle of 45° to within $\frac{1}{2}''$ of the top of the foam (Diagrams 14a and d). The strips of calico are then attached to the top of the foam.

When 1″ plain sheeting is being used for drop-in seats, it is again cut $\frac{1}{2}''$ larger all round than the base. Again it is 'feathered' or tapered at an angle of 45° to within $\frac{1}{2}''$ of the upper surface, but in this case since the foam is 1″ deep, the feathering only extends half-way up the sides of the foam (Diagram 14c).

When the foam is tacked into position the calico is drawn round to the underside of the base. The extra $\frac{1}{2}''$ of foam allows the edge to curve round without danger of splitting.

Cu

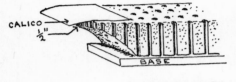

Diagram 14a.
Feathered edge

Diagram 14b.
Feathered edge tacked
down

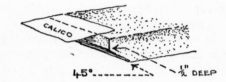

Diagram 14c.
1″ foam feathered

Diagram 14d.
Feathering pin-core
foam

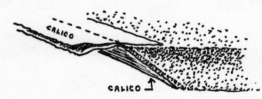

Diagram 14e.
Feathering 1″ solid
foam to a point

To obtain an even edge the calico must be tightened very evenly (Diagram 14b).

Feathering to a Point. This is an extension of the previous type of feathering and is used when upholstering pincushion seats or back insets with plain sheeting. It results in a very gradual rise of the upholstery from the surrounding frame which is the desired effect. The foam is cut $\frac{1}{4}''$ larger than the size of the finished upholstery. It is then feathered at an angle of 30° completely up to the top surface (Diagram 14e).

It is extremely important that the edge of the foam is smooth and unbroken—no little pieces must be snipped out. As the tacks are inserted through the calico along the very edge of the foam, it is the line of the foam which determines the line of the upholstery. The foam is quite thin where it passes over the edge of the frame and so it is strengthened by a strip of calico being attached to the under surface of the foam as well as to the upper surface. Both strips are worked as one piece when being tacked to the frame.

Feathering to a point is also used when feathering doming (Chapter 9 paragraph 4). It ensures that a smooth join results when the doming is placed under an upper layer of foam.

CUSHIONED EDGE (Diagrams 15a and b)

Diagram 15. (a) Cushioned edge. (b) Cushioned edge tacked down

This is very similar in procedure to the feathered edge except that the sides are not tapered but left vertical. This type of edge gives a steeper and firmer edge and is used with most upholstered-over chairs, particularly if they are domed. Again the foam is cut approximately $\frac{1}{2}''$ larger than the frame and the strips of calico are attached to the upper surface. With deeper foam the border is extended to $\frac{3}{4}''$ or $1''$. The extra $\frac{1}{2}''-1''$ of foam around the border is tucked under as the tacking proceeds, and this gives extra strength and support at the edge of the frame (Diagrams 15a and b).

SQUARE EDGE (*Diagrams 16a, b and c*)

This edge gives a very tailored finish and usually the cover has a piped edge and a box side. It is particularly suitable when making round or oval stools.

If pin-core foam or polyether foam is being used the foam is cut very slightly larger than the base on which it is to fit. This means that the foam will be slightly compressed when attached to the base and when the cover is fitted. The cover is always cut to the measurements of the base with suitable allowance for turnings. If cavity foam is being used it must be WALLED to give a firm edge to the finished upholstery. $\frac{1}{2}''$ plain sheeting is used for walling (Diagram 16b). The cavity foam is cut $\frac{1}{4}''-\frac{3}{8}''$ less than the size of the base. A strip of $\frac{1}{2}''$ plain sheeting is then cut the depth of the cavity foam and sufficient in length to go round the cavity foam without being stretched. If the base is round, oval or kidney-shaped, this strip may be cut in one piece or joined. If the base is square or rectangular, then each side of the foam must be walled separately. Care must be taken when cutting walling for square or rectangular units, as two pieces are cut the size of the sides they are to fit. The other two pieces must be $1''$ larger than their respective sides, as they will be attached after the adjacent sides have been built up.

To fix the walling, a thin layer of adhesive is spread over both surfaces. Care must be taken that the adhesive does not go into the cavities or the walling will be drawn into these and a wavy edge will be formed. The walling must be fitted carefully into position; any stretching will distort the cavity foam. The top edge of the walling must be perfectly level with the top surface of the foam. Dust the joints with french chalk.

With all square edges the calico strips are attached to the lower inch of the vertical wall. The calico is then tacked to the edge or underside of the base (See Diagrams 16a, b and c.)

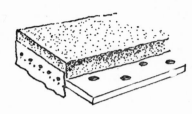

Diagram 16. Different applications of a square edge
a. Solid foam

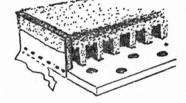

16b. Cavity foam—edge walled

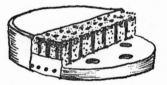

16c. Pin core—no walling

⋆ 5 ⋆

Stools

(Photographs 1 and 2)

THERE IS A tremendous variety in the design of stools. They vary in method of construction, in the type of edge used, and in the base on which they are built. However, to thoroughly master the techniques employed in making a stool is to be well equipped to tackle with confidence a much more ambitious piece of work. This is particularly true of foam upholstery where the principle of foam attached to wood by means of calico is a basic technique employed in the simplest stool or the most elaborate chair or settee.

A stool may be made on a frame or a solid piece of wood. In this chapter those made on a solid base will be described. Those made on a webbed frame are worked exactly as a drop-in seat, except that 2″ foam is used instead of 1″ solid foam.

CONTEMPORARY STOOL

This modern looking stool has many uses. Its removable legs enable it to be easily stored or packed into the boot of a car for picnics etc. It may be covered by any modern woven material but its simple clean lines make the easily cleaned plastic-coated materials particularly practical covering fabrics.

Materials
½″ plywood 11″ × 19″
2″ foam 12″ × 20″

} These measurements may be varied, provided the foam is 1″ larger in each direction than the base

$\frac{2}{3}$ yd. unbleached calico
$\frac{1}{2}$ yd. wadding
1 set contemporary legs and screws
$\frac{1}{2}$ yd. covering material
$\frac{1}{3}$ yd. lining
Dunlop upholstery adhesive 107
$\frac{3}{8}''$ fine tacks

Method

1. Mark mid-points of the four sides of the wood and join to form a cross.
2. Bore $\frac{1}{2}''$ ventilation holes in the plywood at 4" intervals (Diagram 18b).
3. Tear two strips of calico 3" × 24" and two strips 3" × 16". Iron well.
4. Feather all round the foam to within $\frac{1}{2}''$ of the top edge. (See Diagrams 14a and d.)
5. Mark $1\frac{1}{2}''$ border all round the top (i.e. the unfeathered surface) of the foam and spread this border THINLY with adhesive.   (See Diagram 17.)

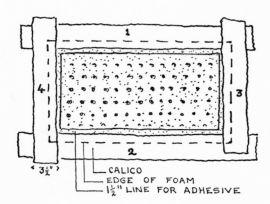

Diagram 17. The method and order of applying calico

$3\frac{1}{2}''$ — CALICO — EDGE OF FOAM — $1\frac{1}{2}''$ LINE FOR ADHESIVE

6. Mark a line $1\frac{1}{4}''$ from one torn edge of each piece of calico. Spread adhesive on this $1\frac{1}{4}''$ border.

N.B. To ensure a smooth flat join it is very important that the fluffy torn edge is covered with adhesive. After spreading, keep the calico quite flat and the edge must not be allowed to roll.

7. When the adhesive has gone dull it will be tacky and the two surfaces may be put together, i.e. foam and calico.

    Take one long strip, hold tightly stretched between the hands and lower on to the foam so that the ink line of Stage 5 can still be seen. There will then be no danger of the edge of the calico not sticking. If this does occur it may roll up and leave an unsightly line visible under the cover which in turn will collect dirt and eventually wear through the cover. Place on the second long strip and then the two short strips (Diagram 17). Leave the corners free—they will not stick down where the overlap occurs.

8. Remove any excess stickiness with french chalk or talcum powder.

To Attach the Foam to the Wooden Base

9. Mark the mid-point of each side of the foam and continue the mark across the calico.

10. Place the foam with the calicoed surface on to the table, and place the wooden base on the top of it, taking care to match the mid-points of foam and wood (paragraphs 1 and 9). The $\frac{1}{2}''$ border will then be evenly arranged all round the board.

11. Turn the calico over on to the underside of one long edge of the board and put in temporary tacks. Turn the stool around and draw the calico over on to the other long side. The extra $\frac{1}{2}''$ of foam is tucked under the base; this gives a rounded edge without any danger of the foam splitting. The line where the foam and the calico meet must come to the edge of the base. The foam must NEVER come over the edge of the wood or the sharpness of the line will be lost (Diagram 14b).

12. Commencing in the centre and working towards the side, completely tack both long sides. The tacks should be $\frac{1}{2}''$ to $\frac{3}{4}''$ apart and about $\frac{1}{2}''$ in from the edge of the wood.
N.B. Remove the temporary tacks before commencing the permanent tacking of the second long side.

Corners—Stage 1

13. Slash calico to the corner of the wood and open the slashed portion outwards. (See Diagrams 18a and 18b.)

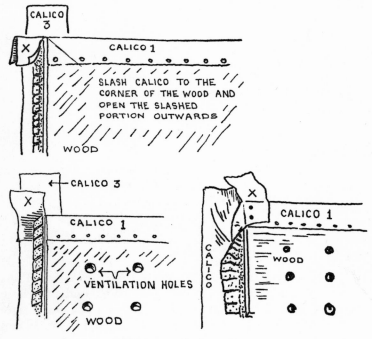

Diagrams 18a, b, and c

14. Turn over this opened-out piece of calico (marked ×) and tack back on to the board. Trim off ALL surplus calico (Diagram 18c).

15. The short sides. Bring the short pieces of calico over to the underside of the base and again working from the centre points, tack to the corners.

Corners—Stage 2

16. Slash the calico as for Stage 1 (Diagram 18a). Open out this slashed calico and bring over the end at approximately 45°. Adjust the angle of the calico so that there are no puckers in it. Mark the edge of this piece of calico on the underlayer of calico and spread with adhesive (Diagram 18d).

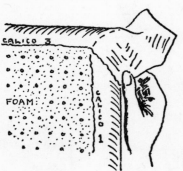

Diagram 18d

Replace the top calico when the adhesive is tacky. Press into position and take the end of the calico under the base and secure with two tacks. Do not turn in any raw edges or surplus material—this causes unwanted bulk. Trim off all surplus.

17. If using pin-core foam, cut a piece of wadding to fit over the upholstery.

18. Put calico over the top of the stool and fasten with temporary tacks on the underside of the base at the centres of the two long sides.
19. Tack along one long side to within 3″ of the corner. The grain of the fabric should follow the edge of the wood.
20. *To Tighten the Cover.* THIS IS ONE OF THE MOST IMPORTANT PROCESSES. Remove the temporary tacks from the second long side. Stroke the cover VERY FIRMLY with the palm of the hand from the tacked edge to the opposite side and over the edge and tack (Diagram 19). Stroke

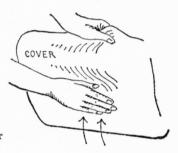

Diagram 19. Tightening cover

in a similar manner before putting in each tack. If the cover is insufficiently tightened it will wrinkle in wear. Never pull with the fingers or a bumpy uneven edge will result. If the cover is too tight there will be shadowed lines showing, running inwards from the tacks—these are known as 'tack draws'.

N.B. This tightening of the cover will bring the foam down on to the base; until this stage it will balloon away from the wooden base.

21. Tack the sides in exactly the same way—stroking outwards from the middle of the stool, and tacking to within $2\frac{1}{2}″$–$3″$ from the corners. Leave the corners untacked.

43

TOP COVER

22. Place this in position—centralizing the pattern and balancing the stripes if necessary. The selvedge must run parallel to the short sides.
23. Tack as for the undercover. There will be less fullness to remove with this cover as the calico is taking the strain of the foam.

Corners

24. Take the points of the undercover and cover and bring over the corner. Pull away from the corner and put in a tack not more than $\frac{1}{2}''$ from the corner of the base. This will give shape to the cover and the grain of the material will begin to fall away under the base (Diagram 20a).

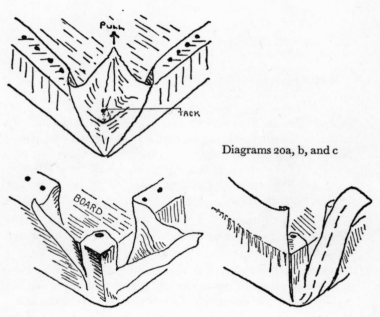

Diagrams 20a, b, and c

25. Fold the material from the sides neatly over the tack and press firmly with the base of the thumb. (The result will be very bulky.)

26. Open out the material and cut to within $\frac{1}{4}''$ of the creases and round the tack (Diagram 20b). Remove the surplus fabric.

Refold material from the long edge and tack into position. Trim away surplus material. Similarly complete the tacking of the side edge. Finish the other three corners (Diagram 20c).

LINING

27. Cut the lining $\frac{1}{2}''$ larger than the wood ($11\frac{1}{2}'' \times 19\frac{1}{2}''$). Turn under $\frac{1}{2}''$ turning ($10\frac{1}{2}'' \times 18\frac{1}{2}''$) and press with an iron. Open out the material and cut off the corner diagonally $\frac{1}{8}''$ from corner creases (Diagram 21a).

Fold over $\frac{1}{8}''$ (Diagram 21b). Refold edges to give mitred corners (Diagram 21c).

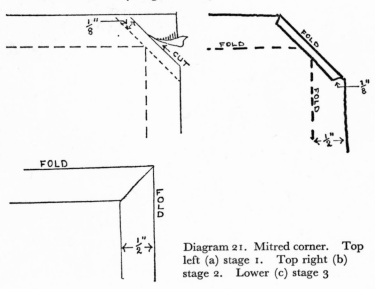

Diagram 21. Mitred corner. Top left (a) stage 1. Top right (b) stage 2. Lower (c) stage 3

45

28. Place the lining on to the underside of the stool. Insert a tack at each corner, keeping the lining very taut. Put in further tacks approximately 1″ apart.
29. Position the legs approximately 1½″ from the corners of the stool. Mark the positions of the screws and pierce the base with a bradawl before putting in the screws.

 N.B. Some of the legs are bought ready stained and polished. If the legs are in their natural state they should be sanded, stained and finished either with wax and polish or one of the modern polyurethane stains.

TRADITIONAL STOOL

This is a particularly elegant type of stool. The size of the base and the height of the legs can be varied according to individual requirements. This style of leg is obtainable in heights ranging from 4″ to 18″. As they have to be fixed to the base before the upholstery is begun the method of upholstery has to be modified from that used for the Contemporary Stool. At the corners it is impossible to take the calico and covering fabric to the underside of the base and so they have to be tacked to the edge of the wood. For this reason the base must be no thinner than ¾″. This allows the tacks to be fixed into the wood with less risk of splitting.

Materials for Small Footstool
¾″ blockboard 10″ × 15″
2″ foam 11″ × 16″
4″ OR 6″ Queen Anne style legs
½ yd. wadding
½ yd. calico
½ yd. covering fabric
⅓ yd. lining material
1½ yds. of gimp or braid (not less than ½″ wide)
12 screws
⅜″ fine tacks
Adhesive

To assemble Stool

1. Mark the centre points of each side of the base. Bore $\frac{1}{2}''$ holes in the base for ventilation.
2. Fix the legs to the base with glue and screws. The corner of each leg fits exactly to corner of the base. The screws pass through the base and into the leg.
3. Prepare the foam as for the Contemporary Stool (paragraphs 3–9). The calico strips for this stool will measure $3'' \times 20''$ and $3'' \times 15''$.

Attaching the Foam

4. Place the foam with calico surface on the table. Put the base of the stool on to the foam—matching the centre points of the foam and the base.
5. Bring the calico to the underside of the stool on the four sides and fasten with a temporary tack at the mid-point of each side.
6. Slash the calico at points A and B up to the edge of the foam. Repeat this on each of the other edges of the stool (Diagram 22a).
7. Tighten the calico, making sure that the foam does not creep over the edge of the wood. Tack between points A and B, first on the two long sides and then on the two short sides.
8. Turn the stool on to one of its long sides. Complete the tacking of one end of the calico on the opposite long side by smoothing the foam towards the edge of the base, and tacking into the edge of the base. Keep the tacks in the upper half of the edge of the base (Diagram 22b).
9. Turn the stool so that the short side is uppermost. Tuck in the spare foam on the side and bring down the end of the long piece of calico diagonally to the short side. Test if the corner of the wood is well padded. It may be necessary to add a little extra padding under the foam. The scraps left from feathering can be used for this. Tack the calico to the edge of the wood. Do NOT pull it

47

down too tightly or the foam will be nipped and the smooth edge to the upholstery will be lost (Diagram 22c). Trim away all surplus calico. Complete the other 3 ends of the long strips of calico.

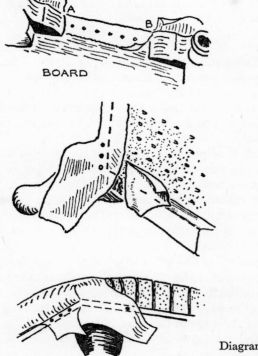

Diagram 22a, b, and c

10. Complete the short sides in a similar way but stick the ends of the calico where they overlap the long strips of calico in addition to securing with the tacks.

Attaching the Undercover

11. Cut and place a layer of wadding over the foam.
12. Place the calico over the wadding and temporarily tack to the underside of the stool at the centre of both long sides.
13. Slash the calico between the legs on the first long side and tack into position on the underside of the stool.
14. Turn the stool around, remove the temporary tack and slash the calico between the legs on this second long side. Tighten by firmly smoothing the calico from the side already tacked. (See paragraph 20, page 43.)
15. Slash the calico between the legs of both short sides and tack into place. Leave the corners untacked.

Attaching the Cover

16. Attach this exactly as the calico undercover.

Corners

The undercover and top cover are worked together from this point.
17. Take the corners of both fabrics and pull downwards over the corner of the stool. Divide the fulness equally on each side of the corner and push this temporarily away from the corner. Put in tacks 1 and 2 (Figure 23a) $\frac{1}{4}''-\frac{1}{2}''$ from the corner of the wood.

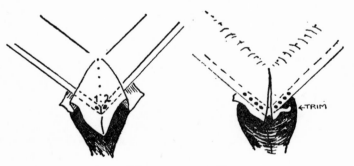

Diagrams 23a and b

18. Turn the stool on to one long side, and working from the inside of the leg, tack the covers to the edge of the wood. Tighten the covers by smoothing the material down towards the edge of the wood, but watch the line of the upholstery carefully for under or over tightening. Keep the tacks towards the lower half of the base so that they will be covered by the gimp or braid.

19. Bring the fulness towards the corner in the form of a pleat and secure with a tack. (This will cover the tack of paragraph 17 above.) Work the other side of the corner similarly (Diagram 23b).

20. Complete all the corners. The two pleats at each corner will face the corner and each other. Trim away all surplus material very neatly.

Attaching the Lining

21. Make a template of the base and from this cut out the lining with $\frac{1}{2}''$ turnings (Diagram 24a).

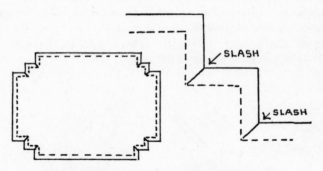

Diagrams 24a and b (enlargement of one corner)

22. Snip at the inside corners of the legs, turn under $\frac{1}{2}''$ and press (Diagram 24b).

23. Place on the underside of the stool and tack into position.

Attaching the Gimp or Braid

This must cover the raw edges where the material has been trimmed away at the top of the legs. The lower edge of the braid should be just below the edge of the base.

24. Spread the underside of the braid with a thin layer of an adhesive such as Clear Bostik or Uhu. Leave the end 1″ untreated.

25. Attach this braid to the edge of the stool, commencing ½″ from one corner, and the 1″ extending unattached.

26. To neaten the final corner trim off both ends of the braid to ½″. Turn in this ½″ and anchor with adhesive. Strengthen the join with blind stitching (Diagram 50, page 88).

When scroll gimp is used, matching gimp pins can be used in addition to the adhesive to give extra security.

KIDNEY-SHAPED DRESSING STOOL

This stool can be made with contemporary or traditional Queen Anne style legs. It is most successful if made with a square edge. The cover is then made with a box-side and the top edge neatened by piping. The stool with contemporary legs can have a fitted or a loose removable cover, and when a loose cover is made this usually has a frill as in Photograph 2A.

Materials

1 Kidney Shape—in ¾″ blockboard for use with Queen Anne style legs

or

—in ½″ plywood with modern style legs.
Maximum overall size 20¼″ × 14½″

1 Set Legs—15″ with appropriate screws.
Foam—2″ pin core or polyether 21″ × 15″

      2″ cavity 20″ × 14″
      ½″ solid foam 60″ × 2″ (for walling)
      ½″ solid foam 17″ × 11″ (for doming)
1 yd. calico
¾ yd. wadding
¾ yd. covering fabric 48″ wide for fitted cover
   or
2¼ yds. covering fabric 48″ for skirted loose cover.
2–4 yds. nylon cord
1¾ yds. gimp or braid for fitted cover.

Preparation

1. If using Queen Anne legs attach them to the base—see Traditional Foot Stool (paragraph 2, page 47).
2. Cut two paper templates of the base and reduce one by 2″ all round the edge.
3. Bore ½″ holes at 4″ intervals in the base.

Preparation of Foam

4. Using the larger template:
    (*a*) With pin-core foam or polyether foam cut out the size of the template plus ¼″ border all the way round. (The doming takes up this extra ¼″ even though the stool has a square edge.)
    Cut the surplus foam into half, i.e. pieces 1″ thick, and use this to build up doming to fit the smaller template. (See Method, Chapter 9, paragraph 4, Diagrams 45b and c.)

    or

    (*b*) With cavity foam cut out ¼″ smaller than the template and wall up with the strip of ½″ solid foam. (See Walling for Square Edge—Diagram 16b). Using the smaller template cut out doming from the piece of $\frac{1}{2}''$ solid $17'' \times 11''$.

N.B. In both cases great care must be taken to keep the scissors vertical when cutting the foam.

5. Attach the doming foam to the underside of the larger shape.

6. Tear a strip of calico approximately $60'' \times 2\frac{1}{2}''$. Iron. (If necessary two or more strips can be used and placed edge to edge on the foam).

7. Put layer of adhesive on the lower $1\frac{1}{4}''$ of the edge of the large kidney shape and on $1''$ of the strip of calico. When tacky place the two surfaces together. Take GREAT CARE not to constrict the foam with the calico—otherwise the foam will be too small to fit on the base (Diagram 25).

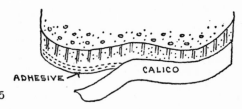

ADHESIVE   CALICO

Diagram 25

Upholstering the Stool

8. Place the foam on the table with the doming uppermost. Place the base on to the foam and put four temporary tacks—north, south, east and west—to attach the calico to the edge of the blockboard.

9. Tighten the calico at these four points, check that the edge of the foam comes exactly to the edge of the wood. Keeping all the tacks in the upper half of the edge of the blockboard, complete the tacking round the edge—continually checking the line of the finished upholstery. If the calico is overtightened or unevenly tightened, the result will be a wavy edge.

53

One function of this undercover is to bring the foam back to the shape of the base as it will have spread slightly when tacked to the base.

10. Using the large template cut a piece of wadding to fit over the top of the stool. Fasten in position at the four opposite points with spots of adhesive.

11. Again using the large template mark the outline on calico and cut $\frac{1}{2}''$ outside this line. The marked line will then be the MACHINING LINE. (See Diagram 26a.)

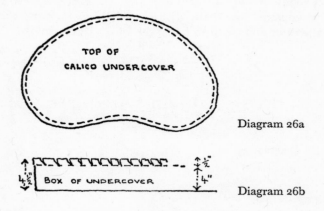

Diagram 26a

Diagram 26b

12. Cut a strip of calico $4\frac{1}{2}''$ deep by the perimeter of the stool plus $1''$—this may be joined if necessary. Machine $\frac{1}{2}''$ from one long edge and slash this $\frac{1}{2}''$ turning every inch. This ensures that the box will fit smoothly round the curved edge of the top section (Diagram 26b).

13. Fix the box round the kidney shape pinning on the marked lines. Join the ends of the box. Baste and machine, again on the marked line. Trim the turnings to $\frac{1}{4}''$.

14. Slip this cover over the upholstered stool and with the

54

hand fit the seam exactly to the edge of the foam. The trimmed seam should face downwards towards the wooden base. If allowed to sit on top of the upholstery it will show under the cover when the stool is in use. Tack to the edge of the base with the tacks a little below the previous row.

Fitted Top Cover

15. Prepare top and the box exactly as for the calico under-cover.

16. Cover the piping cord with crossway strips cut $1\frac{1}{2}''$ wide. Machine tack the cord into the strip using a large stitch, and piping or zipper foot on the machine. Slash every $1''$ right up to the machine stitching. (See Diagrams 4, 6 and 7.)

17. Keeping the material quite flat, fit this piping to the right side of the kidney-shaped top. Pins must be inserted on the machining line of the top and pass between the machine tacking and the cord of the edging. CARE is needed with this operation if the cover is to be a perfect fit.

18. Mark the mid-point of the $48''$ strip of the box. (See Point Y¹, Diagram 27.) Mark mid-point of the convex

CUTTING DIAGRAM .

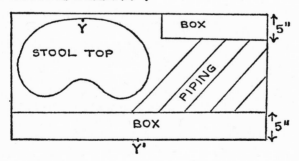

Diagram 27. Fitted cover—cutting diagram

55

side of the top of the cover (Point Y). Fit point Y^1 of the box to point Y on the cover and pin away from this point. The joins of the box section must be balanced about the centre line of the stool and be on the hollow or concave side of the stool (Diagram 28).

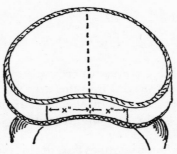

Diagram 28

Machine the seam using zipper foot. Trim away piping cover in the seam to $\frac{1}{8}''$ to give a flat seam.

For Fitted Cover

19. Tack the above cover to the edge of the blockboard, ensuring that the piped edge is exactly on the edge of the stool and that the seam faces down the side of the box. Keep the tacks close to the lower edge of the base. Trim off all surplus material.

20. If using a braid fit this round the lower edge of the stool with pins and pin the join. Machine this join carefully and open out the seam. Spread a thin layer of clear Bostik or Uhu along the edge of the stool.

Slip the braid over the stool and press into position; the join to be in the hollow of the stool.

If using scroll gimp this can be attached with matching gimp pins inserted under the thick 'S'-shaped cords of the scroll.

Frilled Skirt

Prepare the top section as for paragraphs 15–18 of the fitted cover.

Pipe the lower edge of the box and mark half and quarters along the lower edge.

21. Join the sections of the frill.

22. Mark the half and quarters of the frill.

23. Place two rows of gathering threads $\frac{1}{4}''$ and $\frac{1}{2}''$ from the top edge, draw up to the length of the box. Touching or spaced pleats may be substituted for the gathering depending on the material used. Allow twice the length of the box for spaced pleats and three times for touching pleats (Diagrams 54a, b and c).

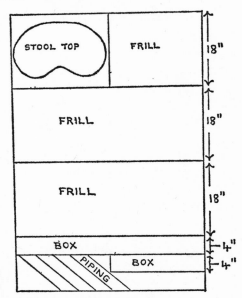

Diagram 29. Frilled loose cover—cutting diagram

24. Fit the frill to the lower edge of the box, matching half and quarter markings. Dispose the fulness evenly. Baste and machine. Trim away the piping covering to $\frac{1}{4}''$.

57

25. Neaten inside edges either with swing-needle machine, binding or by hand.
26. Place over calico cover.   Turn up the hem and stitch.

STOOL WITH SQUARE EDGE
Materials
$\frac{3}{4}''$ blockboard $19\frac{3}{4}'' \times 13\frac{3}{4}''$
Set of $15''$ legs
$2''$ pin-core or polyether foam $20'' \times 14''$

   or

$2''$ cavity foam $19'' \times 13''$
$\frac{1}{2}''$ plain sheet 2 pieces $13'' \times 2''$ ⎫
                 2 pieces $20'' \times 2''$ ⎬ for walling ⎫
$\frac{1}{2}''$ plain sheet for doming $16'' \times 10''$ (optional) ⎭ ⎬

$\frac{1}{2}$ yd. wadding
1 yd. calico
$\frac{1}{2}$ yd. covering fabric, $48''$ wide
2 yds. nylon piping cord
$\frac{3}{8}''$ fine tacks
Adhesive

Preparation
Bore the ventilation holes.   Tear two strips of calico $19\frac{3}{4}'' \times 2''$ and two strips $13\frac{3}{4}'' \times 2''$.   If cavity foam is being used attach the walling.   (See Diagram 16b.)   Fix the doming to the underside of the foam.

Attaching the Foam
With this stool a slightly different method is adopted.   It is essential that the foam fits exactly to the base and that all the edges and particularly the corners are well padded. This is achieved by cutting the foam slightly larger than the base and slightly compressing it.
   1. Place four spots of adhesive at the four corners of the base —on the upper side of the wood.

2. Place adhesive on the four corners of the under-surface of the foam.
3. Allow the adhesive to go tacky and with GREAT CARE fit the corners of the foam over the corners of the base; the foam will balloon slightly.
4. Attach the strips of calico to the lower inch of the sides of the foam, compressing the foam as necessary. If these strips are slightly inaccurate and are attached in the normal way there is a risk that the foam could be distorted, either compressed or stretched. An error of even $\frac{1}{8}''$ can spoil the line of the stool.
5. Tack the calico to the side of the block-board, the tacks being kept near the upper edge, and the calico kept taut. Trim. (See Diagram 16b.)

Calico

6. Cut boxes   2—$20\frac{3}{4}'' \times 3\frac{1}{2}''$
                      2—$14\frac{3}{4}'' \times 3\frac{1}{2}''$
   Cut top section $20\frac{3}{4}'' \times 14\frac{3}{4}''$
   Mark stitching line — $\frac{1}{2}''$ turnings allowed. (See Diagram 30.)

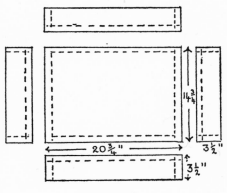

Diagram 30

7. Join the box sections together, machining from the stitching line downwards; i.e. leaving the top $\frac{1}{2}''$ unjoined. The commencement of the machining must be very secure. Open the seams and press.

8. Fit the box to the top section, machine and trim the seam to $\frac{1}{4}''$.

9. Fit over the upholstery. This cover will be tight and will compress the foam, restoring the stool to the dimensions of the base. The joins of the calico must be on the edge of the foam and the seam allowance facing down the box.

Cover

10. Baste the box sections firmly together. Test over the stool for fit—it may be necessary to make a slight allowance as two layers of calico have been added all round the base. Machine as for calico box.

11. Pin the piping to the right side of the top section, slashing it at the corners. Join the ends of the piping and baste. (Diagrams 7a and b.)

12. Fit the box to the top of the cover, pinning the corners first. Machine and trim the seam. Slide this on to the stool and tack to the edge of the base, the tacks being near the lower edge of the wood. Trim off surplus fabric. Neaten with braid or gimp as for the Traditional Stool. Attach the lining and legs.

★ 6 ★

Drop-in Seats

(Photograph 3)

THIS IS ONE of the most common types of seat for stools or chairs; it is found particularly in dining-rooms. As its name implies, the upholstered part of the seat lifts out of its wooden frame, and to re-upholster this is a comparatively simple operation. Usually this type of seat has developed a large hollow in the centre; due either to the webbing having stretched or broken or to the fact that the stuffing has moved from the middle of the seat to the edges.

Type of Foam Used. In the description of the types of foam available in Chapter 1, it is seen that one of the main types of foam produced is known as plain or solid sheeting. This type has the maximum amount of rubber for any given depth, and it is most suited to the drop-in seat. If 2″ cavity or pin-core foam is used, to give sufficient comfort, the centre of the chair will stand too high above the surrounding frame and so spoil the line of the chair. If, however, 1″ cavity is used, the balance of the chair will be correct but there will be too little rubber in the seat to give a comfortable result.

The foam should be a medium to firm density and should be tested for this quality before being bought. It is not usual to dome this type of chair, but this is decided by the original design of the chair. If doming is necessary, ½″ solid foam gives a very satisfactory result.

Covering Materials. Usually this type of chair is subjected to very heavy wear and this should be considered when buying material. The fabric chosen should be closely woven and be recommended for upholstery purposes.   Upholstery tweeds, tapestries, cut and uncut moquette, leather and the modern plastic-coated fabrics are particularly suited to this type of chair, and will give long service.

Most chairs require slightly more than $\frac{1}{2}$ yd. of material in depth, and so it is necessary to buy $\frac{5}{8}$ yd.   This amount will, however, cover two chairs as it is generally 48″–50″ wide. $1\frac{1}{8}$ yds. is usually sufficient to cover a set of four chairs.   It is, however, important to verify these quantities before purchasing.   The seat must be measured after the upholstery has been done, and the selvedge of the fabric should pass from the front to the back of the seat.   Extra material may be needed if the material has a large design.

A VITAL consideration when buying covering material for drop-in seats is to compare the thickness of the proposed new material with that which has been removed.   If a much thicker fabric is used it may be found that the seat may not in fact 'drop in'.   Any modification necessary must be made when preparing the frame.

Preparation of the Frame.   The old cover and upholstery must be carefully stripped away.   (See Chapter 3, Diagram 8.)   When this is completed, the frame, particularly the edges, should be rubbed down with sand-paper.   Any adjustment to the size of the frame must also be made.

If a thicker fabric is being used to cover the seat, the edges of the frame should be slightly planed down.   If, however, a thinner material is being used the edges may need to be built up.   This can be done by glueing and tacking strips of cardboard or linoleum to the edges of the frame.

Webbing.   When webbing the frame of a drop-in seat, it is usual to have three webs of $1\frac{1}{2}″$ Pirelli webbing from back to front and two across the frame, attached by $\frac{5}{8}″$ improved tacks.

Method

Flat Frame (Diagrams 11a and b).   If one side of the frame has a bevelled edge, this is the side which is webbed.

1. Mark centre back and centre front. Tack the webbing to centre back of frame with the edge of the webbing $\frac{1}{4}"-\frac{1}{2}"$ from the edge, using three $\frac{5}{8}"$ improved tacks.

2. Bring to the front edge, stretching one-tenth of its length. (See Chapter 3, Diagrams 9a and b.) Cut off with the scissors held at an angle to give a sloping cut.

3. Attach two side strips of webbing. These will have to divide the spaces between the central strip and the sides —hence they will be closer together at the back than the front.

4. Weave in and tack the two horizontal strips, again stretching one-tenth of their length.

Curved Frame (Diagram 12). In some chairs the seat has a hollowed shape, produced by the curve of the front and back bars. This requires the method of webbing to be modified. The webs passing from the front to the back, i.e. parallel to the straight side, are stretched in the normal manner.

The horizontal webs are woven into place but they are not stretched or the curved shape of the seat would be lost. It is necessary for these horizontal webbing strips to be inserted, even though they are not stretched. They prevent the foam being cut by the sharp unbroken edge of the frame.

Preparation of the Foam

5. Place the frame on the 1″ solid foam and draw round it. Draw a second line $\frac{1}{2}"$ outside this line and cut on the second line.

6. Feather the foam to $\frac{1}{2}"$: i.e. half-way down the foam (Diagram 14c).

7. Apply strips of calico as for the contemporary stool (Diagram 17).

8. Upholster exactly as for the contemporary stool except that no wadding or undercover are required with this type of foam (Diagram 31).

It is ESSENTIAL that no foam creeps over the edge of the

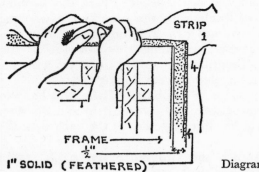

STRIP 1

4

FRAME $\frac{1}{2}$"

I" SOLID (FEATHERED)

Diagram 31

wood—otherwise the frame will not 'drop in' the chair.
N.B. The foam will balloon away from the webbing
until the cover is attached, but the cover will bring the
foam down on to the webbing and give the seat its final
shape.
9. Neaten the under side of the frame with hessian or lining.

STOOLS WITH LARGE DROP-IN SEATS (*Photograph 4*)

These are upholstered in a similar way to the drop-in
dining chair seat, but more webs are required. The long
strips of webbing are fixed in position first. The shorter
strips are then woven into position and spaced $1\frac{1}{2}$"–2"
apart (Diagram 32a). For these larger seats it may be

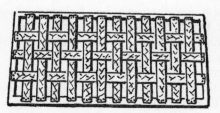

Diagram 32a. Webbing a large base

advisable to dome the seat with $\frac{1}{2}''$ solid foam. The $1''$ solid foam is cut out in the normal way, $\frac{1}{2}''$ larger all the way round than the frame.

To dome the seat cut the doming of $\frac{1}{2}''$ solid foam $2''-2\frac{1}{2}''$ less all the way round. This is attached to the underside of the $1''$ solid by spots of adhesive at the four corners (Diagram 32b).

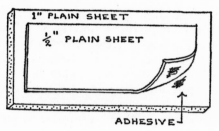

Diagram 32b

REMOVABLE INSETS IN CHAIR BACKS (*Photograph 7*)

This type of back is comparatively rare—the more usual type being the pincushion type (Chapter 7). When it does occur it is usually upholstered on a removable piece of solid wood, which must have ventilation holes bored into it. It is then upholstered in exactly the same way as the drop-in dining chair seat.

★ 7 ★

Pincushion Stuffed Seats
(Photograph 5)

THIS TYPE OF seat is frequently found on very delicate types of chairs and stools, and so a great deal of care is needed both when stripping and re-upholstering such a piece of furniture. The actual upholstery is very quickly done, but its very simplicity demands an extremely high standard of workmanship.

The upholstery is secured to a very narrow rebated strip of the frame. The narrow and delicate strip has to take the webbing and its tacks, the foam and its tacks; also the cover and its tacks. This will indicate why such care is necessary. In this type of seat as with the drop-in seat, the aim is a very gradual rise in the upholstery, and so 1" plain sheet foam is used.

Preparing the Chair

When the chair is being stripped the polished wooden surround should be protected by an old cloth, in case the stripping chisel slips. The large number of holes left by the removed tacks should be filled with plastic wood. This is necessary so that the new tacks will find a firm base when hammered into position. When the plastic wood is firm the whole of the unpolished wood should be rubbed down with sandpaper.

Webbing the Seat

When attaching the webbing two faults must be avoided.
1. The webbing must not be allowed to give a bumpy outline to the finished upholstery.

66

2. Suitable tacks must be used to avoid splitting the wood.

Method

Usually three webs from front to back and two from side to side are sufficient. The webs from back to front must be fixed so that they are equally spaced: i.e. they will be closer together at the back than the front.

Attach the webbing with three $\frac{1}{2}''$ improved tacks or clout nails, if the frame will permit; or two $\frac{1}{2}''$ tacks and three $\frac{3}{8}''$ improved tacks if there is danger of splitting. Cut off the webbing about $\frac{1}{4}''$ from the inside edge of the rebate.

To avoid an uneven outline—cut pieces of cardboard the thickness of the webbing. Stick these to the wood between the webbing. (See Diagram 33 below.)

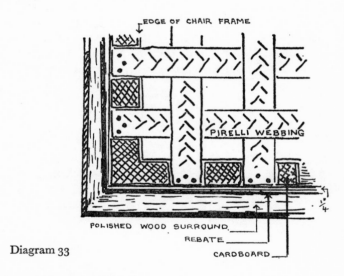

Diagram 33

Preparing and Attaching the Foam

1. Make a template to fit inside the rebate—trim off $\frac{1}{4}''$ all round.
2. Cut $1''$ plain sheet foam to fit this template.

3. Feather VERY CAREFULLY to a point. The feathering should be at an angle of about 30° (Diagram 14e, page 34).
4. Tear eight strips of calico 2" wide—two strips are used for each edge—allow 1" spare at each end of the strips.
5. Stick four strips of calico to the top of the foam, attaching the front and back strips first (Diagram 17). Then stick the other four strips to the underside of the foam in the same order—these reach to the edge of the feathering. The thin feathered edge is sandwiched between the two layers of calico and is given extra strength where it sits on the wooden frame.
6. Tack to the chair frame, working the two pieces of calico as one piece. The tacks MUST go in along the very edge of the foam. The line of tacks MUST be exactly parallel to the edge of the rebate. (See Diagram 34.) This is the MOST IMPORTANT STAGE of the work as these tacks determine the line of the finished upholstery.
7. Trim off all the surplus calico. (See Diagram 34.)

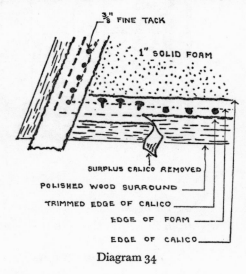

Diagram 34

8. Place the cover material over the upholstery centralizing the pattern if necessary.

9. Temporary tack the cover at the centre back and front, also at the centres of the sides. When tacking the cover into position none of the tacks are fully driven into position until the whole of the tacking is completed. Often they have to be removed to allow the material to be smoothed out at the corners, or to allow the raw edges to be turned in after trimming.

10. Commencing from the centre, tack along the front edge to within $2"-2\frac{1}{2}"$ of the corner.

11. With the palm of the hand smooth the covering material firmly towards the back edge and tack in a similar way.

12. Tack the sides, again to within $2"-2\frac{1}{2}"$ of the corner.

13. Smooth the material diagonally outwards at the corners and tack, adjusting those tacks already in position if necessary.

14. If the covering material is not too thick trim it to within $\frac{1}{2}"$ of the tacks. Remove the tacks one side at a time. Turn in the $\frac{1}{2}"$, retack, and mitre the material at the corners. If the material is thick or the rebate very shallow—hammer in the tacks already in position, and trim the material with very sharp scissors or a razor blade.

Trimming

15. The edge of the upholstery can be neatened with scroll gimp, a flat upholstery braid, or metal headed studs. The latter are rather heavy for delicate furniture and this should be considered before deciding to use them. When attaching braid or gimp, commence at one back corner and leave $\frac{1}{2}"$ spare to trim off just before joining, as these materials are very liable to fray.

Gimp may be attached using matching gimp pins or by a combination of adhesive and gimp pins. The scroll on one edge of gimp is deeper than the other. Have the deeper scroll towards the inside of the chair and temporary tack at one back corner so that the outer edge of the gimp overlaps on to the wooden surround. The raw or folded edge of the covering fabric will then be completely hidden.

Take the gimp to the next corner and stick or tack into position. It will then follow a perfectly straight line— if it is tacked gradually from one corner to the next the result may be a bent or wavy line. Put in intervening tacks about 1″ apart so that they are hidden by the scroll. When hammering pins into position lift the scroll carefully out of the way so that it is not cut by the hammer. If using braid it is usually wise to stick it and use gimp pins only at the corners.

To neaten the ends of the gimp or braid, trim off to $\frac{1}{4}$″. Fasten down the beginning of the braid, fold under the $\frac{1}{2}$″ at the other end and secure over the raw end with a spot of adhesive. Place in final gimp pins. Complete the underside of the chair with lining.

PIANO STOOL TOP

The tops of these stools frequently are upholstered with a pincushion type seat, but often it is built over a solid base and so the task is much simpler.

Ventilation holes must be bored into the base and then the upholstery is completed as for the above chair.

Neatening

As the framework is usually heavier on these stools, metal studs can well be used to neaten the edge of the covering fabric. They must be placed in position very accurately if they are to give a professional finish and a template should be made as suggested in Chapter 2, Diagram 3.

PINCUSHION INSETS (Photograph 6, left)

These are the type usually found in the back of chairs. It is rarely necessary to use webbing as there is little strain on them. Sufficient support is given by tacking a piece of material to the front of the frame over the hole. If the back of the upholstery can be seen through the hole from the back of the chair then a piece of covering material, with its right side to the chair, should be used.

Alternatively a piece of hessian or lining material can be used, and in this case the back of the chair is neatened with a piece of covering material.

The inset is then upholstered as the pincushion seat, but $\frac{1}{2}''$ solid sheet is used instead of $1''$ unless a very deep pad is required.

CHAIRS WITH THE REBATE DAMAGED

This is a very common problem encountered when this type of chair has been upholstered and re-upholstered. The wood of the rebate is incapable of supporting the webbing even though the holes are filled with plastic wood. In this case the webbing may be attached to the underside of the seat. An extra piece of $1''$–$1\frac{1}{2}''$ foam is cut to fit into the hollow of the seat. This foam should be slightly thicker than the wood. The rest of the upholstery is then attached in the normal way (Diagram 35).

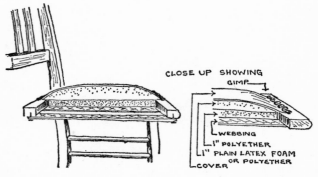

CLOSE UP SHOWING
GIMP

WEBBING
1" POLYETHER
1" PLAIN LATEX FOAM
COVER OR POLYETHER

Diagram 35. Cross-section, showing pin-cushion seat webbed under frame

* 8 *

Upholstered-over Chairs
(Photographs 6, 7 and 8)

THIS TITLE IS given to chairs where the upholstery covers the whole of the top of the seat and the cover is carried down the sides of the chair. This cover may completely cover the sides and be fastened underneath the frame, or it may extend to a polished band of wood round the lower edge of the seat. Taking the upholstery over the edge of the frame is the method best suited to repairing a previously cane seated chair, and is also used when the chair has a removable seat held in position by the back uprights and a central peg on the front of the frame as in Photograph No. 7.

Frequently this type of chair has had a sprung base, but if the springs are not in perfect condition, they can be replaced with Pirelli webbing. The result will be equally comfortable and will give many years of hard wear.

When chairs are stripped in the usual way it may be found that the base of the seats vary. The top of the seat may be perfectly flat or the tops of the front legs may extend above the level of the rest of the seat (Diagram 41a). The method of upholstering each type is given below.

CHAIR WITH FLAT SEAT
Materials
1½"–2" Pirelli webbing
2" pin-core or cavity foam or Polyether foam
1" solid foam—optional doming
1 yd. calico

72

⅝ yd–¾ yd.–1 yd. of covering fabric, depending on whether
the cover is taken underneath the frame

1 yd. wadding

⅜″ fine and ⅝″ improved tacks

Adhesive

Webbing the Seat

The webbing is done in the usual way but as the seats are
larger than most drop-in frames, it will probably be necessary
to use five webs from back to front and three horizontally.
For larger chairs each web should be stretched one-eighth of
its length. The webbing is always attached to the top of the
frame. If the chair previously had a sprung base, the old
webbing would have been attached to the underside of the
frame. When the springs are dispensed with and replaced
by Pirelli webbing this is tacked to the top of the frame of the
seat.

Preparing the Foam

1. Cut a template of the seat.
2. Cut out 2″ foam ½″ larger all round than the template, but
   DO NOT CUT OUT THE CORNERS AT THE BACK (Diagram 36).

Diagram 36

3. If doming is required cut this out of 1″ solid foam 2″ less
   all round than the template—feather this to a point and
   fix to the underside of the 2″ foam by a thin layer of
   adhesive.

73

4. Calico the foam as shown in the Diagram 37 below—noting that the calico does not extend to the back corners.
5. Mark the centre back and centre front of both the foam and the chair.
   Place the foam over the Pirelli webbing matching the centre points.
6. Roll the foam over and bring the calico down over the front of the frame to give a cushioned edge. (See Diagrams 15a and b.) No foam must come over the edge of the seat. Temporary tack and repeat at the back of the seat.

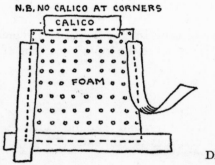

N.B. NO CALICO AT CORNERS

CALICO

FOAM

Diagram 37

7. Carefully roll the extra foam under and permanently tack the calico strip to the front edge of the frame about ½″ below the top edge. Keep the calico pulled well down at the corners and finish these as for the traditional stool (Diagrams 22b and 22c) and add extra padding if necessary at the corners.
8. Put in three tacks along the back edge. Where the foam puckers at each back upright slash it diagonally—do NOT cut any foam away. The extra foam is compressed against the wooden support and will later trap the undercover and cover, and so hold it in position—complete the back tacking.

9. Tack the sides—again finishing as for Traditional Stool.
10. Cover with wadding. If the cover is taken under the chair, the wadding should extend under the chair to pad the sharp edges of the frame.
11. Place the calico undercover over the wadding and secure at the centre back and front with temporary tacks. Tack along the front edge, or under the front edge (depending on the type of chair) to within 3″ of each corner.
12. Smooth the cover towards the back edge to tighten it and put in three tacks only along the back edge.
13. Fold the calico back diagonally from the back upright so that the fold *just* touches the wood. Slash diagonally to within ½″ of the wooden upright. Test for fit and snip again if necessary. (See Diagram 38.)

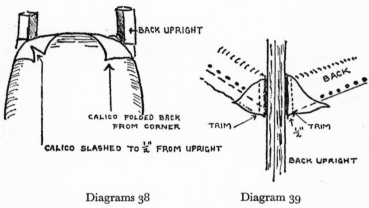

Diagrams 38   Diagram 39

14. Turn the flaps of the spare material outward so that the fold JUST touches the back upright. Trim to within ½″ of the fold. Lift up the material, turn the ½″ underneath and complete the tacking of the back. The ½″ should be gripped between the foam and the wooden upright. (See paragraph 8, above and Diagram 39.)

15. Commencing at the centre tack the sides. Tack up to the back upright but only to within 3" of the front corners.
16. At one front corner lift the material where there is fulness and slash inwards to the end of this fulness. Lap one flap over the other and tack down into position. This prevents a pleat being formed under the top cover. (Diagram 40.)

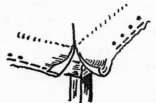

Diagram 40

17. Fix the top cover exactly as the undercover to Stage 16: i.e. the front corners. These are now finished as the corners of the Traditional Stool (Chapter 5, Diagrams 23a and 23b).
18. If the chair has a polished lower edge to the seat the covering material is trimmed to $\frac{1}{2}$" and the raw edges turned in, or if the covering material is thick, it is trimmed back to $\frac{1}{8}$" below the tacks. In both cases braid or gimp is used to neaten the edge. If the cover is taken underneath the chair the material over the front leg is trimmed to $\frac{1}{2}$" below the level of the seat, turned in and secured with matching gimp pins.
19. Line the underside of the chair with hessian or black linen.

CHAIR WITH EXTENDED FRONT LEGS

In this case an extra template is made cutting out the corners at the back uprights and the extended front legs. This is cut out of 1" plain sheeting (Diagram 41b). A layer of adhesive is spread on the top of the seat frame and on to the under edge of the foam. When tacky the foam is placed over the seat, and the top of the foam should then be level with the top of the front legs (Diagrams 41a and 41b).

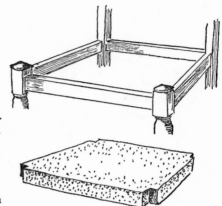

Diagram 41a. Frame show-
ing extended front legs

41b. 1″ solid foam

If this foam is omitted the tops of the legs will cut through the 2″ foam and also an uneven front edge will be obtained. The upholstery is then completed as in paragraphs 1–19: but the calico strips for paragraph 4 must be 1″ deeper.

CHAIR WITH SQUARE EDGE (*Photograph 6, left*)

1. When using this method it is advisable to use the doming foam. Cut the 2″ foam ¼″ larger all round than the seat, attach the doming to the underside.
2. Attach the corners of the foam to the seat of the chair with spots of adhesive. (See Stool with Square Edge, page 58, paragraphs 1–3.) Attach the calico strips as for the stool and tack into position (page 59, paragraph 4). Apply the wadding and undercover, turning them over the square edge, and cutting out the surplus material at

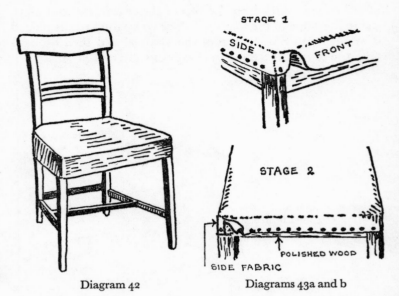

Diagram 42   Diagrams 43a and b

the front corners.   The raw edges should meet edge to edge at the front corners.   (Attach as in paragraphs 11–15 of the previous chair.)

Top Cover

Fix as in the previous method, except for the front corners. Bring the front edge of the side material round to the front and put in a tack $\frac{1}{2}''$ from the corner (Diagram 43a).   Fold the surplus material underneath and crease.   Cut away to within $\frac{1}{4}''$ of the crease and tack.   Fold the front material over the cut edge and tack (Diagram 43b).   (If the covering material is thick it may be necessary to put a thin layer of wadding along the front between the two cut edges.   If this is necessary the wadding should be thinned away along the top edge so that no ridge is produced.)   The pleat so formed should be stitched down with blind stitching (Diagram 50, page 88).

CANE SEATED CHAIR (*Photograph 8*)

As is suggested at the beginning of the chapter (page 72), this method of upholstering a chair is best suited to chairs previously cane seated. The webbing should be attached between the line of the holes left by the cane and the outer edge of the frame.

If the webbing is attached too close to the cane-holes, splitting is likely to occur. After webbing the chair is upholstered as for the chair with the flat seat frame (see page 73). The foam and covering materials are tacked to the edge of the seat and neatened with gimp or braid.

Alternatively these chairs may be upholstered as a 'Pincushion' type chair with a damaged rebate and webbed underneath the seat (page 71). In this case the upholstery is taken just outside the line of the holes and the polished surround left visible (Diagram 35).

★ 9 ★

Upholstered Bentwood Chairs
(Photograph 9)

THIS TYPE OF chair, although not originally designed to be upholstered, can be converted into a delightful occasional chair for very little cost. If the legs are shortened these chairs when upholstered look particularly well in a bedroom. They can be upholstered with the same material as that used for the curtains or for a fitted bedcover. Bentwood chairs have been easily obtainable in sale rooms for as little as half-a-crown. Many are still available although now the cost may have risen.

Normally when the back of a chair is to be upholstered, there is a rail between the back uprights, parallel to the seat and about 1″ to 3″ above the top of the seat. (See Diagrams 68, 71, 72.) When converting a bentwood chair, there is no such rail and so the normal method of upholstering the back of a chair has to be modified. This can be done most successfully. Some of these bentwood chairs have a curved piece of wood running from the lower part of each back upright to each side of the seat. This can safely be removed and this should be done to improve the shape of the completed upholstery. The legs may be reduced in height so that the seat of the chair is 12″ to 13″ from the floor but the height can be varied to suit individual needs (Diagram 44).

If the centre of the seat is a solid piece of wood and in good condition, ventilation holes must be bored through it. If the central wood is damaged the base of the seat can be webbed using the same method as for the top ring of the Humpty. (See Diagram 58.)

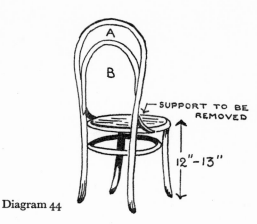

SUPPORT TO BE REMOVED

12"-13"

Diagram 44

Materials

$1\frac{1}{2}$" foam 18" × 18" (seat)   ⎫ These may vary according to
$1\frac{1}{2}$" foam 18" × 20" (back)   ⎰ the size of the chair
$2\frac{1}{4}$ yds. of 48" upholstery fabric
2   yds. calico
$2\frac{1}{2}$ yds. wadding
$1\frac{1}{2}$ yds.–2 yds. Pirelli webbing
$1\frac{1}{2}$ yds. flat braid or gimp (minimum width $\frac{1}{2}$") or piping cord
Tacks and adhesive

Preparation of Foam

1. Make a paper template of the seat, taking the paper right to the edge of the chair.
   Make a template of the back, shaping the paper well into the curve of the chair.
2. Using the 20" × 18" foam, cut out the back shape 1" larger all round than the template. This extra 1" allows the foam to roll over the edge of the wooden frame. Feather the lower edge only.
3. Place the template of the seat on the 18" × 18" foam as shown in Diagram 45a. Cut out $\frac{1}{2}$" all round larger than the template.

Fu

4. Reduce the template of the seat by $1\frac{1}{2}''$ all round. Take the spare pieces of foam A, B, C, and D left from the seat and stick together (Diagram 45b). Place over the smaller template and trim. Using all the spare pieces of foam build up and complete second circle (Diagram 45c).

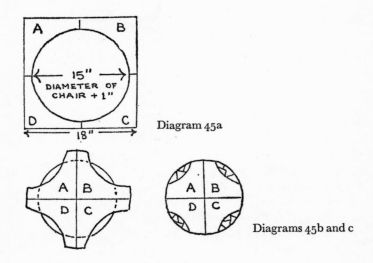

Diagram 45a

Diagrams 45b and c

Feather this circle to a point (Diagram 14e) and it will be used for the doming.

Even though the foam used was only $1\frac{1}{2}''$ thick the completed seat will be 3″ deep. This method of making the doming is economical, and at the same time produces a comfortable seat with a pleasing line. The original bentwood seat is concave, and the completed seat should have a convex outline.

5. Mark the exact centre of both circles and attach these together by putting a spot of adhesive on both centre points.

6. Tear strips of calico 4″ wide and attach these to the

seat and back sections of foam as shown in Diagrams 46a and 46b). (Note there is no calico on the seat foam where it will touch the back uprights.)

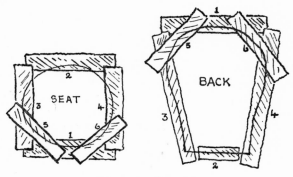

Diagrams 46a and b

Upholstering the Seat

7. Place the foam on to the chair seat with the doming to the base of the seat. Temporary tack the calico to the side of the chair seat at the centre back and centre front.
8. Commencing at the centre of the front strip of calico (i.e.

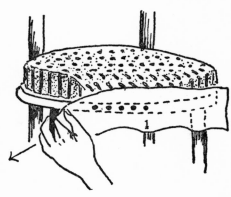

Diagram 47. To avoid confusion only one strip is shown

83

strip No. 1) tack the foam to the edge of the chair. Keep the tacks about $\frac{1}{4}''$ from the top edge of the wood. Draw the ends of the calico down tightly so that it meets the wood at an angle (Diagram 47). Trim away surplus calico. Tack the back, and the sides in a similar way—starting always from the centre of the strip of calico. Lastly the diagonal strips at the front are tacked to complete the shaping. Where these overlap the front and side strips they are stuck down with adhesive.

Attaching the Undercover

9. Cut a square of wadding and place it over the foam. Cover this with calico and temporary tack at the centre front and centre back.
10. Tack about $4''$ to $5''$ along the centre front. Tack about $\frac{1}{2}''$ below the top rim and about $1''$ apart—do not drive the tacks in at this stage as they may have to be adjusted later. Smooth firmly towards the back to tighten the calico and tack about $3''$ at the centre of the back.
11. Slash the calico at the back uprights as for the Upholstered-over Chair (Diagrams 38 and 39). Complete the tacking of the back strip.
12. Tack the sides of the cover working outwards from the centre of the side. Complete the tacking of the cover up to the back uprights.
13. At the side fronts there will be some fulness. Slash to the end of this fulness and lay one piece of calico over the other. (See Diagram 40.) Tack into position, adjusting any tacks along the front edge if necessary.

Attaching the Cover

This is attached exactly as the undercover except for the treatment of the fulness at the side fronts. The tacks securing the cover are about $\frac{1}{4}''$ from the lower rim of the chair. Care must be taken that the motifs are centralized if the material is patterned.

14. Side front fulness: Divide this fulness equally into two—smoothing diagonally outwards. Place a tack between the two sections of fulness. Divide the fulness a second time and tack, then four pleats can be formed all facing the corners: i.e. two will face to the right and two to the left. Trim off all the surplus (Diagrams 48a and b).

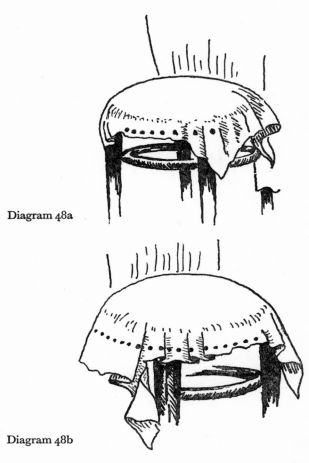

Diagram 48a

Diagram 48b

To Upholster the Back

15. Tack three pieces of webbing to the front of the top rail of the chair—cut these off so they reach the bottom of the seat but do not tack the lower edges (Diagram 49).

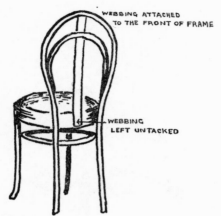

Diagram 49

If these were tacked at this stage no further materials could be taken through to the back—this is the effect of there being no tack rail. (See page 80.)

16. Place back foam in position and temporarily tack at the centre bottom, at the centre of the top, and centre sides. It should roll well over the sides and top without any stretching, and will probably appear too large at this stage.

17. Tack down all the strips of calico except the bottom strip in the same order as they were attached to the foam. Keep the tacks well to the back of the frame.

18. Cover with wadding and calico. Remove the temporary tack holding the strip of calico at the bottom of the foam in position. Tack the central 4″ to 5″ at the top of the calico undercover. Smooth the calico down towards the seat and cut at the two uprights, so that the

86

fly may be pushed through to the back of the seat. Tighten this quite strongly and secure with three or four temporary tacks. This will give the back its shape—causing it to curve inwards. Some vertical puckers will inevitably appear but these will disappear as the sides of the calico are tacked into position.

19. Tack the side—commencing at the centre and only smoothing the cover sufficiently to remove the puckers produced in Stage 18. Over-tightening at this stage will result in the loss of the curved shape of the back.

    All tacks should be kept as far to the back as possible so that they will not cut through the top cover.

20. At the top corners slash along the fulness and overlap the pieces of calico as on the seat. Complete the tacking.

Attaching the Cover

21. Place the material over the back of the chair. If the material has a pattern, the motifs on the seat and on the back should match. Cut to the required size.

22. Remove the temporary tacks securing the bottom of the undercover to the seat.

    Tack the central 4″ to 5″ of the top of the cover, to the back of the chair, but do not drive in the tacks fully. Smooth the cover down the front of the chair towards the junction of the seat and the back. Slash towards the centre of each upright, cutting to within ½″ of the back of the chair.

23. Push the fly at the bottom of the cover through to the back and tighten the cover to restore the shape to the back upholstery. Tack this to the back of the seat.

24. Retighten the calico undercover and secure to the back edge of the seat—also secure the strip at the lower edge of the foam (Strip No. 2, Diagram 46b).

25. Now take a pair of pincers or pliers and stretch the Pirelli webbing. Fasten the bottom of each strip to the

back edge of the seat with three $\frac{5}{8}''$ improved tacks.

26. Complete the tacking of the cover as for the undercover. The fulness at the top corners is disposed of in small downward-facing pleats.

27. Tack double layer of wadding over the outside back. This gives a smooth finish and adds strength to the back cover.

28. Cut and pin the outside back into position. Trim to $\frac{1}{2}''$. Turn in this $\frac{1}{2}''$ and secure with dressmaking pins. Fasten with blind stitching at the top and sides (Diagram 50). Tack to the underside of the seat at the bottom edge.

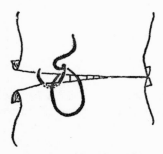

Diagram 50. Blind stitching

FOR SHALLOW-BUTTONED BACK

This is upholstered exactly as for a smooth back except that no Pirelli webbing is attached to the front of the frame: i.e. Stage 15 is omitted. Work Stages 16–26, and proceed as follows:

1. Working from the back of the chair, make templates of the inner spaces of the frame of the chair: i.e. (A and B, Diagram 44).

2. Cut out these templates in 1″ polyether foam. Fit these into position attaching them with adhesive to the foam already upholstered to the chair.

3. Cover the buttons and determine their positions on the front of the chair.

4. Attach three or five pieces of webbing to the back of the chair. These pieces of webbing are attached in the normal way, being stretched as they are attached. The positions of the buttons will determine the number and placing of the webs as a piece of webbing must always be behind a button.

5. These webs will tend to balloon away from the chair, so one strip of webbing is placed across the hollow of the chair back to restore the shape. It is not interwoven (Diagram 51).

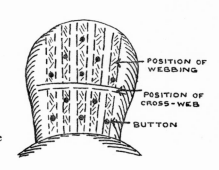

POSITION OF WEBBING

POSITION OF CROSS-WEB

BUTTON

Diagram 51. To show possible design for buttons

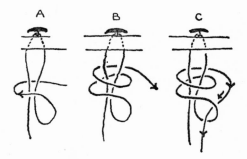

Diagram 52.
Upholsterer's knot

6. Using a 6″ to 8″ mattress needle, fix the buttons in position. Secure each button with an upholsterer's knot (Diagram 52). Slide a piece of glove leather between

the knot and the webbing. This prevents the twine cutting the webbing.

Complete the back as for the unbuttoned chair.

The Edge of the Seat of the Chair

This may be neatened by a frill and braid, or gimp, or simply by braid. In the latter case the legs may be stained or painted.

The braid or gimp can be stuck on with clear Bostik or Uhu. With a scroll gimp, gimp pins of a matching colour can be used, and these are hidden under the S-shaped scroll. The join should be in a hollow, where one back upright meets the seat. Each cut end should be folded back under itself, stuck into position and the two folded ends pushed together to form a 'butt-joint' (Diagram 53).

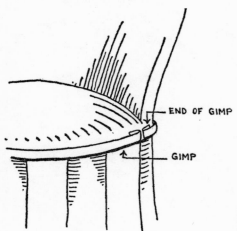

Diagram 53. Butt-join of braid or gimp

The ends can then be made thoroughly secure by putting two gimp pins into each end.

TO MAKE A FRILL

To make the frill with spaced pleats gives a pleasing finish which is not too heavy in appearance or too expensive in material.

This method requires a strip of material twice the circumference of the chair. 3″ pleats and spaces give a well-balanced effect (Diagrams 54a and b). If the material has stripes or motifs these will require special thought and the pleating will need modifying to suit the particular design (Diagram 54c).

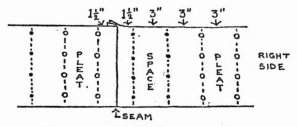

Diagram 54a. Making four 3 spaced pleats

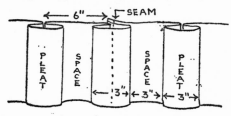

Diagram 54b. Frill pleated

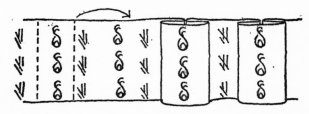

Diagram 54c. Pleating based on the design of fabric

Cutting the Material for the Frill

1. Measure from the top of the wooden base of the seat to the floor and allow $1\frac{1}{2}''$ for a hem.
2. Cut sufficient strips of material to allow for twice the circumference plus generous turnings at the joins. Two widths of 48" materials are rarely sufficient. The seats of most bentwood chairs have a circumference of at least 51" to 52".

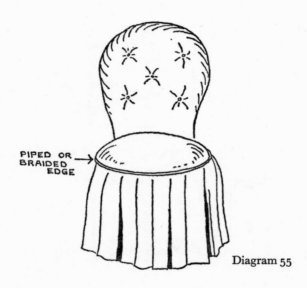

PIPED OR BRAIDED EDGE →

Diagram 55

3. Join two strips of material together with a single seam. Do not press the seam open. Mark the top edge as in the Diagram 54a—commencing by marking $1\frac{1}{2}''$ either side of the seam and then every 3".
4. Make the pleats so that the join disappears in a pleat, and continue pleating to form 3" pleats and 3" spaces.
5. Measure the length of the frill and add a third length if necessary—ensuring that again the join comes under a

pleat. Complete the pleating and join the ends of the frill to form a continuous strip.

6. Machine $\frac{1}{8}''$ and $\frac{3}{8}''$ from the top edge. Neaten the lower edge either with a swing needle machine or Paris binding.

7. Place the frill in position, with a pleat at the centre front. Tack into position with the tacks fitting between the two rows of machining.

Neaten the top of the frill with a gimp or a braid as for the chair without the frill (page 90).

Check the length—the lower edge of the frill should be $\frac{1}{2}''$ above the floor. Turn up a hem and slip-hem into position.

An alternative finish is to neaten the join of the frill to the chair with piping. The piping is first machined to the top of the frill $\frac{1}{2}''$ from the edge. The frill is then attached to the chair by back-tacking. (See paragraph 13, page 138, Diagrams 84 and 91.)

★ 10 ★

Pouffe

(Photograph 2b)

THIS POUFFE HAS been designed so that it is quite firm and stable and yet not so heavy that it is difficult to move—a fault common to many pouffes. This lightness is achieved by having the central cavity completely empty and enclosed by a strip of calico which forms a support for the side uphol-stery. The blockboard used for the base and upper ring is sufficiently heavy to give the stability necessary.

The measurements given below, both for the diameter and the height of the pouffe, can be varied to suit individual requirements. If the diameter exceeds 14″ two extra struts of 1″ dowelling should be used.

Materials

2 circles of $\frac{3}{4}$″ blockboard 14″ diameter
6 lengths of 1″ dowelling—10″ each
12 screws—2″ eights
17″ × 17″—1$\frac{1}{2}$″ foam. Pin-core or polyether

or

16″ × 16″—1$\frac{1}{2}$″ cavity foam plus $\frac{1}{2}$″ solid 2″ × 46″
51″ × 13″—1″ polyether foam
1$\frac{1}{3}$ yds. calico 48″ wide
1 yd. covering fabric 48″ wide
$\frac{1}{2}$ yd. wadding
$\frac{1}{2}$ yd. hessian
4$\frac{1}{2}$′ Pirelli webbing 1$\frac{1}{2}$″ wide
$\frac{3}{8}$″ fine and $\frac{5}{8}$″ improved tacks
4 dome feet   Adhesive

1. For the most successful and comfortable result cut out
   an inner circle, diameter 10″, from one piece of blockboard—this will leave a ring 2″ wide. If the supplying
   shop will not do this and difficulty is experienced use
   one of the following simple 'do-it-yourself' methods.

   (*a*) Draw the inner circle of 10″ to leave a 2″ ring. Drill
   a hole with $\frac{1}{4}$″ bit. Insert a fret-saw blade through
   the hole. Tighten the blade into the saw and cut
   along the marked line.

   N.B. Fret-saw attachments are obtainable for many
   power drills.

   or

   (*b*) Draw the inner circle as above. Using $\frac{1}{4}$″ or $\frac{3}{8}$″ bit
   drill holes as shown in Diagram 56. Make these holes

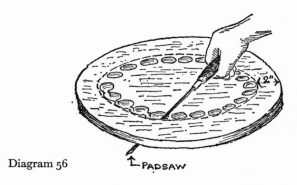

Diagram 56   ⌐PADSAW

as close as possible for easy cutting: The principle is
that of perforated paper. Cut between the holes with a
key-hole type of saw until the central portion of wood
can be removed.

The top piece of blockboard can be left solid, but the
resulting seat is much less comfortable. If solid blockboard is used, ventilation holes must be bored through
it.

2. Fix the six pieces of dowelling into position between the two pieces of blockboard, using glue and screws. The screws pass through the blockboard into the dowelling. (See Diagram 57.)

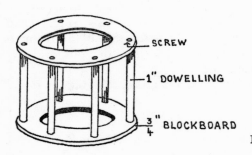

SCREW

1" DOWELLING

$\frac{3}{4}$" BLOCKBOARD

Diagram 57

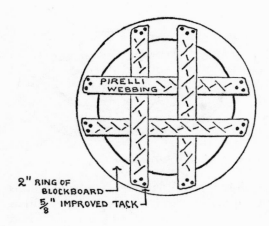

PIRELLI WEBBING

2" RING OF BLOCKBOARD

$\frac{5}{8}$" IMPROVED TACK

Diagram 58

Webbing the Top Ring

3. Web the top ring with four strips of Pirelli webbing—stretching each strip one-tenth of its length (Diagram 58).

96

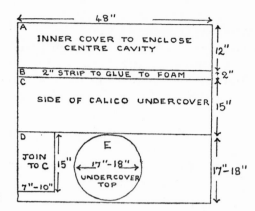

Diagram 59

Preparation of the Foam

4. Mark a circle, diameter $14\frac{1}{2}''$, in the centre of the $17''$ square of foam. The doming will lift the top foam— hence the allowance of the extra $\frac{1}{2}''$. Cut out, keeping the edge vertical.

   If using cavity foam, this circle must be cut $1''$ smaller; i.e., $13\frac{1}{2}''$ diameter and walled with the strip of $\frac{1}{2}''$ solid foam. (See Walling, Diagram 16b.)

5. Using oddments of foam, A, B, C, D, build up a second circle $10''$ diameter. (See Diagrams 45 a, b, c, Chapter 9, Bentwood Chair.) Feather this circle to a point (Diagram 14e).

6. With adhesive attach the centre of the doming circle to the centre of the $14\frac{1}{2}''$ circle.

7. Mark line $1\frac{1}{4}''$ from the lower edge of the $14\frac{1}{2}''$ circle and spread with adhesive. Mark $1''$ from the long torn edge of the $2''$ strip of calico (Strip B, Diagram 59) and spread with adhesive.

8. When the adhesive is tacky place the calico around the vertical edge of the $14\frac{1}{2}''$ circle taking great care not to

Gu

97

constrict the foam—otherwise it will not fit on to the frame.   (See Diagram 25.)

Attaching the Foam

9. Mark, north, south, east and west of the top ring of the frame and of the foam.
10. Place the foam on to the frame, matching the above marks.   Temporary tack into the side of the top ring.

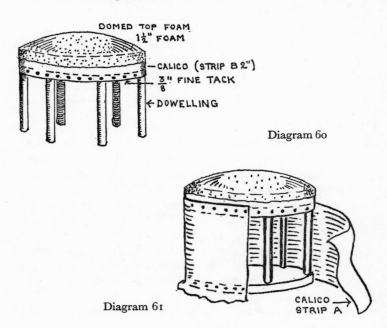

DOMED TOP FOAM
1½" FOAM
— CALICO (STRIP B 2")
⅜" FINE TACK
← DOWELLING

Diagram 60

Diagram 61

CALICO →
STRIP A

11. Tack the lower 1″ of calico to the edge of the blockboard—tacks about 1″ apart and going into the upper half of the edge of the blockboard (Diagram 60).   Care must be taken that the edge of the foam comes exactly to the edge of the frame, and that the calico is kept taut. Trim away any surplus calico.

12. Take strip A of the calico and tack to the edge of the top ring of the blockboard. There will be some overlap at the end.

13. Tighten the calico towards the bottom of the frame and tack (Diagram 61). Trim the overlap to 2″ and stick into position.

    This calico will give a firm side to the pouffe, enclose the hollow central cavity and form a support for the foam used to upholster the side of the pouffe.

14. Feather to a point the top long edge of the strip of 1″ polyether foam.

15. Spread this feathered edge and the bottom 1″ of foam with adhesive. Also spread the top 1″ of the seat foam and the calico over the lower rim of the frame with adhesive—allow to go tacky.

16. Fit the top feathered edge of this side strip to the top edge of the seat, and the lower edge to the bottom rim of the pouffe (Diagram 62).

    Trim away any spare foam at the join and stick.

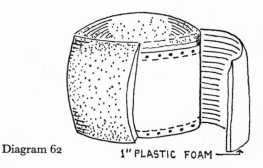

Diagram 62   1″ PLASTIC FOAM

Assembling the Inner Cover

Use strips C and D and circle E of the calico.

17. Join strips C and D with a single seam. Mark $\frac{1}{2}$″ from the top long edge and machine stitch along this line.

99

Slash to the machining every 1". This allows the box to fit smoothly around the circular top section of the cover.

18. Check the size of the circle necessary to cover the pouffe—and allow $\frac{1}{2}"$ seams, Circle E—cut circle of wadding and baste to the calico circle.

19. Baste the strip C/D around circle E, having the join in the strip and the wadded side of the circle outside. Join the side seam of the strip. Baste and machine. Slip this cover over the pouffe. It should fit quite tightly.

20. Turn the lower edge of the calico to the underside of the pouffe. Draw it down tightly but evenly and tack to the underside of the frame. Tacks to be $\frac{1}{4}"$ to $\frac{1}{2}"$ inside the edge. Slash any pleats formed in the calico to give a smooth finish. Trim away surplus material.

The Outer Cover (Diagram 63)

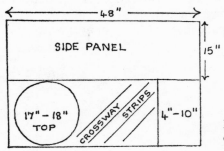

Diagram 63. Cutting diagram for cover fabric

This is made exactly as the inner calico cover but the top edge is neatened either by piping (Diagrams 6 and 7) or a commercial trimming.

Lining the Base

Cut the hessian the size of the base plus $\frac{1}{2}"$ turnings. Machine with a small stitch $\frac{3}{4}"$ from the cut edge. Slash almost to the machining and turn in the raw edge. The slashing will enable the lining to fit smoothly on to the base. Tack into position and fit the small feet to the underside of the pouffe.

★ 11 ★

Boudoir Chair
(Photograph 10)

THIS IS A most delightful chair, suitable for use in the bedroom or as an occasional chair in the living room. It can be used as a sewing or knitting chair.

Webbing

Using 2″ Pirelli webbing, web the base as shown in Diagram 64, stretching the webbing one-eighth of its length. The position of the back uprights prevents five webs being placed from the front to the back of the chair. To overcome this difficulty three webs are attached and then five horizontal webs used to give the necessary strength to the seat (Diagram 64).

STRETCHED WEB

UNSTRETCHED WEB

Diagram 64

Because of the curve of the chair back the webbing of the back does not follow the normal pattern. Commencing at the centre, three webs are attached from the inside of the top rail to the front of the tack rail at the bottom of the chair back. These are stretched one-eighth of their length. Interlaced with these are two horizontal webs, but they are not woven in alternately. Both these webs pass behind the outer vertical webs and in front of the central web; also they are not stretched. This allows the curved shape of the frame to be preserved.

Materials

2″ foam—two pieces for the seat (approx. 21″ × 21″)
1½″ or 2″ foam for the back (approx. 21″ × 21″)
1″ foam for the seat doming 17″ × 17″ (only if cavity foam is being used for the rest of the upholstery)
2″ Pirelli webbing, approx. 6½ yds.
2 yds. calico—48″ wide
1½ yds.–1¾ yds covering fabric—48″ wide
2 yds. piping or commercial fringe to match the cover
⅜″ fine and ⅝″ improved tacks
Adhesive

Cutting the Foam

1. Cut 2 templates of the seat.
2. Fit paper to the back of the chair rolling it to the extreme edge of the top rail—it will be necessary to slash it to allow it to roll over the top of the frame. Take the sides of the paper to the back edge of the side of the frame.
3. Cut out two pieces of foam for the seat—one ⅛″ larger all round and the second ¼″ larger all round than the template.
   With cavity foam each piece will have to be cut out ½″ smaller than the above measurements and walled with ½″ plain sheeting (Diagram 16b).
4. Reduce one template by 2″ all round. If using cavity

foam cut out this smaller shape from the doming foam
(1″ foam 17″ × 17″).

If using plain or pin-core foam cut all scrap foam from
paragraph 3 through the middle to give foam 1″ thick
and build up the doming from this as for the Bentwood
Chair. (See Diagram 45.) Feather doming to a point.

5. Cut out the back from the 1½″ foam allowing 1″ all
round the pattern.

The Seat

6. Using the smaller piece of foam, measure the distance
between the two side supports of the back and tear a
strip of calico the same length and two inches wide.
Tear a second strip to fit round the rest of the frame.
Taking care not to compress the foam, attach these
strips to the lower inch of the side of the foam—to give a
square edge (Diagram 16c).

7. Place this foam on to the webbing and tack to the
side of the seat, the tacks being about 3″ apart (Diagram
65).

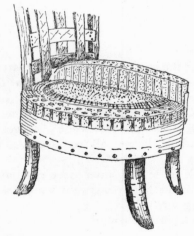

Diagram 65

8. Place the 1″ doming centrally over this foam and attach it with adhesive (Diagram 65).

9. Using the larger piece of foam—tear 4″ strips of calico similar in length to those in Paragraph 6, and attach them to the lower inch of the edge of the foam. Place this foam over the seat and again tack to the side of the seat. Tighten the calico so that the first layer of foam is slightly compressed (Diagram 65).

10. Cut a circle of wadding and stick it to the top of the seat. Cut a strip of wadding 4″ wide to go all round the seat except at the back. Stick it to the lower 3″ of the side of the seat, leaving 1″ to be taken underneath the frame.
    Cut a second strip of wadding 1″ deeper than the combined depth of the foam and the frame—stick this over the first layer to wad the side of the seat completely, again tacking it underneath the frame.

11. Using the template of the seat cut a circle of calico with ½″ turning—mark on this the inside and outside of the back uprights, slash the seam allowance at these points. Cut a box for the cover allowing ½″ turning at the top and 1″ at the lower edge. Divide the box so that one piece will fit the centre back and the other pass round the sides and the front of the chair. There should be 2″ spare material at each end of the larger portion. These ends will be tacked to the back legs.

12. Make up the cover. (See Chapter 5, Kidney-shaped Stool—paragraphs 11 to 13, page 54.)

13. Place the cover over the foam. It will be smaller than the top of the chair so the foam must be compressed in order that the seam of the cover sits on the edge of the chair.

14. Tack the back flap to the back of the seat. Beginning at the centre front tack the rest of the box to the underneath of the frame. Keep the calico taut and slightly compress the foam—keeping the edge of the chair level.

Where the box passes over the front legs it will be necessary to slash the lower edge of the box. With the undercover the surplus material is cut away level with the edge of the seat.

15. Tack the lower 2″ of each end of the long portion of the box to the legs (paragraph 11).

16. Make up the seat cover as the calico cover but neaten the seam with fringe or piping.

   Attach it to the frame as the undercover. The surplus material at the lower edge where the box passes over the front leg is turned in and secured with matching gimp pins.

The Back

17a. Attach calico strips to the back foam.

18a. Place in front of the chair. Take the lower strip to the outside of the tack bar and tack. Bring the foam over the top of the chair and tack along the outside of the top rail. To finish corners see Diagrams 18 a, b and c.

19a. Tack the side strips of calico to the back of the side supports. Finish top corner as Diagram 18d.

20a. Fit wadding and calico over the foam. The calico must be very tight vertically to bring the foam on to the webbing. The lower edge is slashed and the flap taken through to the back, turned upwards and tacked to the tack bar. Overtightening when tacking the sides will cause loss of shape. Finish the top corners of the calico by slashing the fulness. (See paragraph 16, Chapter 8.)

21a. Fit the cover as the undercover. Finish the top corners as for the Contemporary Stool. (Diagrams 20 a, b, and c.)

22a. Bring the material at the lower edge of each side diagonally down to the point where the bottom of the seat meets the back leg. (See Diagram 66.) This will be over the ends of the box of the seat cover. (See paragraph 15.)

23a. Stitch the two materials together with blind stitching, for the bottom 3".

24a. Tack a layer of wadding over the outside back.

25a. Cut the outside back cover—with ½" seam allowance.

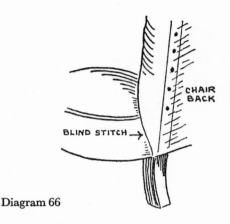

Diagram 66

26a. Secure this by back-tacking to the top edge. (See Chapter 13, Diagram 84.)

27a. Turn in the side allowance and secure with blind stitching. Slash the lower edge so that it can be taken to the underside of the frame between the legs. Turn up the material over the back legs and secure with matching gimp pins.

29a. Line the underside of the chair.

Alternative Treatment of the Back—Squared Edges

Make a template of the back, again taking it to the extreme edge of the back rail, but only to the front edges of the side supports.

17b. Attach calico strips to the upper surface of the foam

at the top and bottom of the foam to make a cushioned edge (page 35, Diagram 15).

At the side attach calico strips (2″ wide) to the edge of the foam as for a square edge (Diagram 16).

18b. At the top and bottom tack the calico to the frame as in 18a.

19b. At the sides tack the calico to the side of the uprights.

20b. Make template of the sides of the chair and cut out of ½″ polyether foam—stick these to the sides of the chair.

21b. Cut wadding to fit the front and side panels of the chair and stick into position.

22b. Cut similar pieces of calico, with ½″ seam allowances. baste the front section to top and front edges of the side sections (Diagram 67a). Machine and fit over the back.

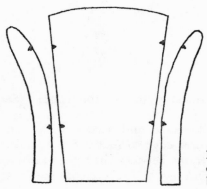

Diagram 67a. Cutting diagram of calico and cover for tailored back

23b. Tack the back edge of the side panels to the outside back of the side supports, the top edge to the outside of the top rail and the lower edge to the tack rail.

24b. Cut the inside back and side panels from the cover fabric.

25b. Make piping to fit round the side panels. Fit this round the panels except at the lower edge (Figure 67b).

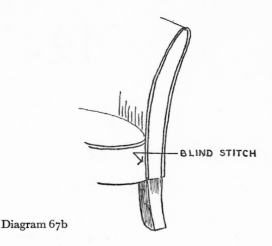

BLIND STITCH

Diagram 67b

26b. Fit the side panels to the front section and machine, using the zipper foot. The cover should fit tightly over the foam (Diagram 67b).

Tack the back edges to the outside of the back frame.

Finish the lower edge as in 20a. Blind stitch the side panel to the seat box, at the lower front edge.

27. Finish the outside back as for the first method (paragraphs 24a–29a).

These frames may be purchased from The Russell Trading Company—see useful addresses, page 150.

★ 12 ★

Victorian Chair
(Photographs 11a and b)

THIS IS ONE of the most rewarding renovations on which a worker can embark. It may appear very ambitious, yet with care and patience a highly professional finish can be achieved.

In many respects the re-upholstery of the back may be compared with that of a pincushion seat. The main differences are that thicker foam is used and it is not feathered at the edge.

As the upholstery of the back is to be attached to a very narrow strip of wood, it is essential to fill all the tack holes in the wood which are left after the stripping has been completed.

Materials

2″ Pirelli webbing
2 pieces 2″ foam for seat
Doming 1″ foam—this may be assembled from scraps of 2″ foam cut in half horizontally or from a piece of 1″ foam
2″ foam for the back
Polyether foam—the depth of the wood of the frame—for padding the back of the frame
Button moulds
2 yds. calico (approx.)
2 yds. covering fabric (approx.)—48″ wide
Braid or gimp
Lining
Tacks   Adhesive   Twine

Preparation

1. Make a template of the seat, taking the paper to the outside of the seat frame.
2. Cut a template of the inside of the back frame. This may be in two pieces. (See Diagram 68, foam marked A.)
3. Fit paper to the front of the back, taking it to the edge of the rebate, and shape it well into the curve of the back. Cut out the template.

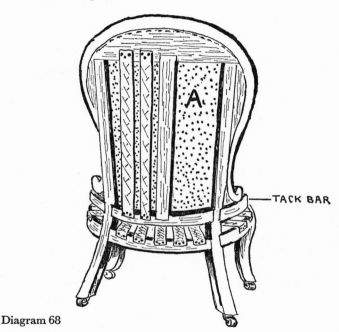

TACK BAR

Diagram 68

Upholstering the Seat

4. *Webbing.* Usually the old webbing was attached to the underside of the seat, and then springs fixed over this. The springs may be dispensed with and the 2″ Pirelli webbing attached to the top of the seat bars. A difficulty

may arise at the back and the sides as the seat bars and the tack bar at the bottom of the back may be close together and therefore not allow the hammer to drive in the tacks. This is overcome by tacking the end of the webbing to the outside back of the seat and bringing the webbing up over the edge of the frame and so to the front of the frame. A small piece of wadding should be placed between the webbing and the edge of the frame to prevent the wood cutting into the webbing (Diagram 69).

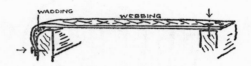

Diagram 69. Cross-section of seat

5. Cut out one piece of foam to the exact size of the template, and attach this as for a square edge (Diagram 16c). No calico should be attached where there are wooden uprights. The foam should not be cut away at the wooden uprights; merely slashed and compressed around the wood.

6. Cut and attach the doming.

7. Cut the second piece of seat foam allowing $\frac{3}{4}''$ to $1''$ all round the foam to give a cushioned edge. Attach calico to the surface of the foam—the strips being $5''$ wide (Diagram 15).

8. Tack the calico to the outside of the seat bars.

9. Cut wadding and calico undercover to fit over the seat. These may be tacked either underneath seat or above a border of polished wood, depending on the design of the chair. It is attached as for the Upholstered-over Chair (Chapter 8, paragraphs 10–16).

10. Fit the cover as the cover of an Upholstered-over Chair. The cover will be slashed wherever there are wooden

uprights; possibly each side of the back and also at the centre back where an extra support passes up the centre of the back.

The lower edge may be neatened by gimp, braid or an upholstery fringe.

Upholstering the Back

11. *Webbing.* The webbing is attached to the outside back of the frame and the vertical webs only attached at this stage. They are stretched one-eighth of their length. (See Diagram 68.)

12. Take the template(s) of the inside of the back—paragraph 2—cut these out of the polyether foam which is the same depth as the wood of the frame, and allow $\frac{1}{4}''$ all round. The foam will be compressed when it is fitted into position.

13. Spread a thin layer of adhesive round the edge of the foam, also on the inside edge of the frame. When tacky place in position—the back of the foam will fit against the webbing.

14. Using the larger template of the back (paragraph 3) cut out the 2″ foam.

Allow 2″ all round except along the lower edge where $\frac{1}{2}''$ is allowed.

15. Lay the foam on a table and mark a line 2″ from the edge of the sides and top. Cut $1\frac{1}{2}''$ either side of this line (Diagram 70a). The scissors will point towards the line, but enter the foam at an angle of 45°. The cut does not go completely through the foam but to within $\frac{1}{2}''$ of the other surface. A triangular wedge of foam is cut out from the three sides (Diagram 70b).

Spread each side of the cut with adhesive—allow this to go tacky and press the two surfaces together. This will give a rolled edge to the foam and produce the required raised edge to the upholstery (Diagram 70c).

Hu

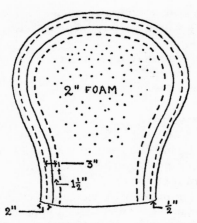

Diagram 70a. Back foam showing wedge to be cut out

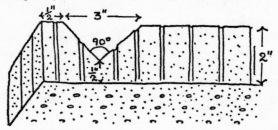

Diagram 70b. Cross-section of foam before sticking

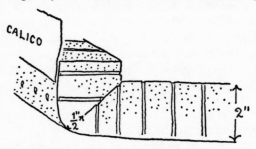

Diagram 70c. Cross-section of foam after sticking

16. Attach 2″ strip of calico to the edge of the foam except at the lower edge (Diagram 70c).
    Attach strip(s) of calico 6″ to 9″ deep to the lower edge. This calico is taken through to the back, turned up over the tack rail, and tacked into position.
17. Tack the narrow calico strip to the front of the rebate, keeping the edge of the foam $\frac{1}{4}$″ to $\frac{1}{2}$″ from the edge of the polished surround. (See Diagram 34 for position of tacks.)
18. Place thin layer of wadding over the foam, holding it in position with spots of adhesive.
19. Cut covering material to fit over the front of the upholstery. Allow a minimum of 6″ to 9″ surplus at the top and sides for the buttoning, depending on the size of the chair. At the lower edge, allowance must be made so that the material can be taken through and tacked to the tack rail. Anchor the cover in position with glass headed pins. (These are easily seen and do not disappear into the foam.) Cover the button moulds with scraps of material. (See Chapter 16—Buttons.)
20. Decide on the position of the buttons. (See Headboard—Chapter 16.)
21. Attach the horizontal webs to the outside of the back of the chair. (See paragraph 4.) These should be positioned so that the buttons are attached over intersections of the webs. These webs need not be interwoven.
22. Commencing from the centre button position, attach the first button. Secure the twine at the back with an upholsterer's knot. (Chapter 9, Diagram 52, paragraph 6). Before tightening the knot slip a piece of glove leather between the knot and the Pirelli webbing.
23. Work outwards from this position—disposing of the fulness in diagonal pleats. (See Chapter 16, Diagram 96, Pages 147–148, Paragraph 14.)
24. When all the buttons are attached, smooth the material

towards the frame and temporary tack at the centre of the top and centre sides.

25. Dispose of fulness at the edges in vertical or horizontal pleats (Diagram 96). Tack the material along the edge of the foam to the wooden rebate (Diagram 34). At the lower edge smooth the cover downwards to the junction of the back and seat. Slash to within $\frac{1}{2}''$ of this crease where there are wooden uprights and draw the flap(s) through to be tacked to the back tack rail.

26. Trim $\frac{1}{8}''$ from the tacks and neaten with gimp or braid (Chapter 7, paragraph 15).

27. Put a double layer of wadding over the outside back and tack.

28. Place the outside back cover in position and tack just inside the upholstery line.

Trim and neaten with braid or gimp.

29. Line the underside of the chair.

⋆ 13 ⋆

Armchair

THE CHAIR WHEN stripped down should be inspected for any attack by insects or for weak joints, and treated if necessary.

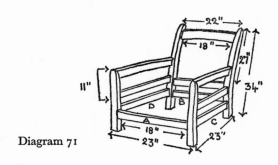

Diagram 71

Measurements are given in this chapter to aid in the identification of relative pieces of foam, but these should be modified to fit each specific chair frame.

Webbing

1. *The Seat.* By using Pirelli webbing it is possible to dispense with the springs. The webbing is attached to the top of the seat bars, A, B, C and D. Depending on the size of the chair 5 to 7 webs of 2″ webbing should be attached from the back bar to the front bar, stretching each web one-eighth of its length. 4 to 5 horizontal webs are woven into these first webs, being concentrated where the maximum weight will fall: i.e. the centre and towards the back of the

117

chair. It may be necessary to attach the webbing at the back to the outside of the frame. (See Diagram 69.)

2. *The Arms*. These webs are attached to the inside of the chair frame. 2″ or 1½″ Pirelli webbing can be used and the webs stretched one-tenth to one-eighth of their length. One web should be attached close to the back leg and 3 to 4 other webs should divide the space between the back and the front of the chair (Diagram 72).

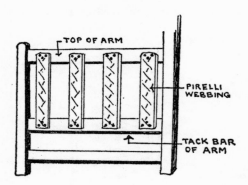

Diagram 72

3. *The Back*. Again the webbing is attached to the inside of the chair. Five vertical webs of 2″ webbing and 4 horizontal webs interwoven with these will give the necessary strength and resilience.

Cutting the Foam. Use medium firm or firm density foam.

The Seat

Cut pieces of foam as in the diagrams opposite.

One or two pieces of Section A are used depending upon the depth of seat required, and the size of the chair.

The Back

The foam for the back is 4″–5″ longer than the frame so that it will roll easily over the top of the chair.

118

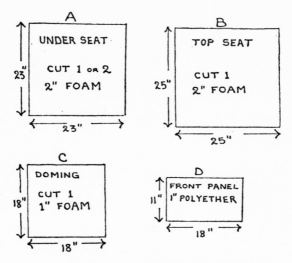

Diagram 73. Cutting diagram for seat foam

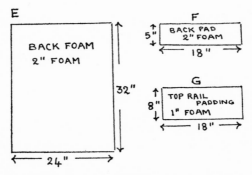

Diagram 74. Cutting diagram for back foam

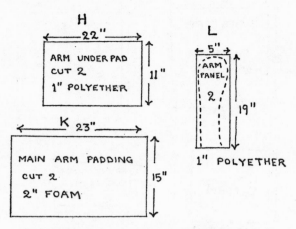

Diagram 75. Cutting diagram for the arm foam

Upholstering the Seat

1. If using two pieces of Section A join these together to give a final depth of 6″ of foam.
2. Tear strips of calico 3″ deep to fit exactly between the legs. Attach these to the lower 1″ of Section A of the foam (Diagram 76).

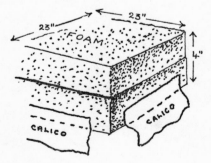

Diagram 76

3. Put this foam on to the Pirelli webbing, and bring the calico strips to the outside of the seat frame. Tack at 3″ intervals.

4. Feather 1″ solid foam (C) to a point (Diagram 14e) and place this over the foam already attached to the frame, ensuring it is exactly in the centre of the chair. Secure at each corner with adhesive.

5. Tear four pieces of calico 9″ deep again to fit exactly between the legs of the chair. Attach these to the top of the largest piece of foam (B) as in Diagram 77. The deep pieces of calico are necessary as they are to go down over the 6″ of foam and to be tacked on to the seat bar.

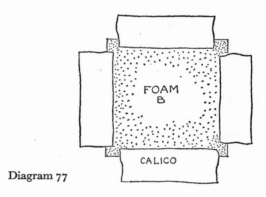

Diagram 77

6. Place this foam over the doming and push the calico strips at the back and sides down between the lower foam and the tack bars. Tack to the seat. Roll the foam at the front to produce a cushioned edge and tack to the front edge of the seat.

7. Feather to a point the top edge of the front panel of 1″ polyether foam (D). Spread the feathered edge and 1″ at the long unfeathered edge with adhesive. Spread with adhesive the front edge of the seat where the front strip of calico joins the foam, and also the calico over the front

of the seat rail. When tacky press the panel into position. This gives a rounded line to the front of the chair and adds comfort.

8. Put a layer of wadding over the seat and tack it to the underside of the seat at the front—this will protect the cover from the sharp edge of the wood.

9. Over the wadding place the calico ensuring that it will pass from the underside of the frame at the front, over the seat and through to the back of the seat. At the sides it must reach to the outside of the seat frame. Temporary tack under the front edge. Stroke towards the back and secure with temporary tacks. Cut each of the four corners as for the back corners of the Upholstered-over chair (Diagram 38, page 75). Trim away surplus calico at the corners (Diagram 39) and put in the final tacks. Leave the calico at the ends of the front panel untacked. Pin and blind stitch these ends to the material going down the side of the seat.

Outer Cover

If the material is limited or very expensive, it is possible to economize by adding flys of inexpensive strong material where they will not be seen—in this case at the back and sides of the seat. The inside back, and the inside arm pieces may be similarly treated. The cover is now attached in a similar manner to the undercover. The front is attached under the frame but the material is left unattached at each end of the front panel, and blind stitched as in para. 9 above.

The Back

10. Spread with adhesive the top edge of the back of the frame and the inside of the top rail—also one side of the top roll foam (Back foam—Section G). When tacky press the foam to the top edge of the back and roll it to the inside of the back—this will give a well upholstered top edge (Diagram 78).

11. Attach a piece of calico to each end of the back support (F) and tack to the sides of the back just below the arms. This will give shape to the chair and fit into the hollow of the back of a person using the chair.

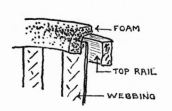

Diagram 78. Cross-section showing top roll of 1″ plain foam

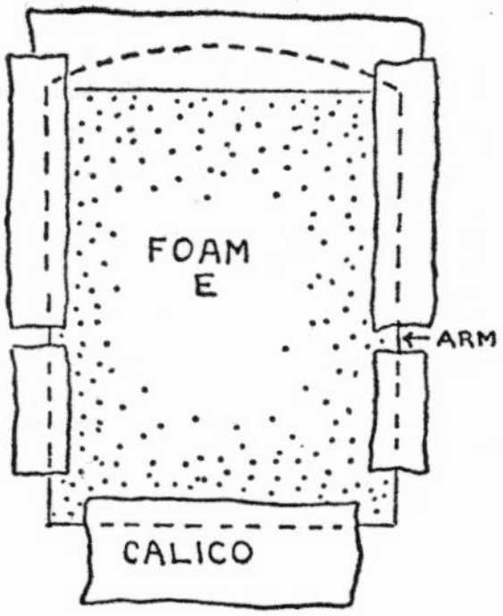

Diagram 79

12. Attach calico to the back foam (E) as shown in Diagram 79.
13. Place the foam in position, draw the bottom strip of calico through to the back, turn it upward and temporary tack to the tack rail at the bottom of the back. Roll the top of the foam over the top of the chair and tack along the outside back of the frame. Finish the corners as for a Contemporary Stool (Diagrams 18a, b, and c).
14. Slash the foam where it meets the arms, but do not cut any foam away. Draw the side strips of calico round to the back of the frame but the foam must not extend beyond the edge of the inside of the back. Complete the tacking, finishing the top corner as shown (Diagram 18d, page 42).
15. Place a layer of wadding over the foam, ensuring that it extends over the top and sides of the chair to the outside of the back.

123

16. Place calico over the wadding. Temporary tack along the top outside back. Tighten by smoothing the calico towards the seat and slashing at the bottom so that the flap will pass through to the outside back. Turn this up over the tack bar and fasten.

17. Fold the sides of the calico inwards and run the hand up the folds so that the creases fit snugly up to the arms. Slash towards the centre of the arm rail and to within $\frac{1}{2}''$ of the wood. Make 'Y' slash (see Diagrams 80 and 81 below) for $\frac{1}{2}''$ and turn in $\frac{1}{2}''$ to $\frac{3}{4}''$ of fabric depending on the thickness of the arm rail. Work the cover around the arm, making extra slash if necessary. Take the calico to the back of the frame and tack.

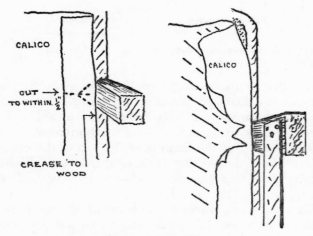

Diagrams 80 and 81

18. Slash any fulness at the top corners and place one piece of calico over the other. (See Diagram 40.) Tack and trim.

19. Fit the outer cover in exactly the same way except for the corners. (See paragraphs 16 and 17.)

20. The top corners are finished as are the corners of a Contemporary Stool.   (See Diagram 20.)

Protect the outer cover with old cloth while upholstering the arms.

The Arms

21. Spread a layer of adhesive along the inside of the top arm rail, and also down the inside edge of the arm.   Spread a 1″ border with adhesive along the top and front of the 1″ polyether foam (Arm Section H).   Press the polyether foam to the inside of the arm.   Stick a strip of calico over the front edge of the foam and on to the frame (Diagram 82).

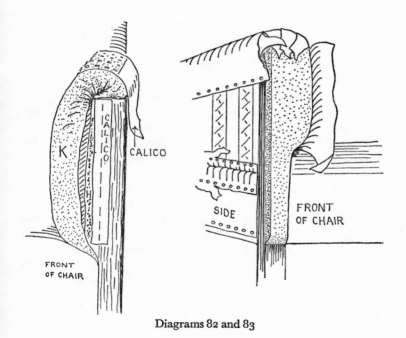

Diagrams 82 and 83

22. Attach 3" strip of calico to the top and front edge of the 2" foam (Section K) also a 6" strip to the lower edge. This strip should measure the distance between the inner edges of the front and back legs and be suitably placed on the foam.

23. Place the foam inside the arm and take the lower calico through between the seat and the arm tack rail. Turn it upwards and tack it to the rail.
   The front edge of the foam MUST be level with the front of the arm.

24. Roll the foam over the top of the arm and tack the calico to the outside of the frame. Where the back of the arm foam meets the back of the chair compress it between the back web on the arm and the upholstery of the back of the chair. The foam will balloon away from the arm at this stage (Diagram 82).

25. Put a layer of wadding over the foam, allowing 1" to extend beyond the foam at the front of the arm.

26. Cut the calico lining to extend from the outside of the lower tack rail to the inside of the arm, over the foam to the outside of the arm. In width it should be 5" to 6" more than the foam. Place this over the foam, leaving 3" to 4" extending beyond the foam at the front of the arm. Slash the lower edge so that it may be secured to the outside of the lower tack rail. Stroke the material firmly up over the arm to the outside of the frame. Care must be taken that the grain of the material is horizontal along the top of the arm. The calico is tacked to the outside of the arm rail. At the back of the arm, the calico is folded inward and slashed level with the bottom of the arm. The flap is then taken to the back of the chair, but not tacked. The calico will have given shape to the arm and it will now be possible to cut the front arm panels.

27. Make a template of the front of the arm and cut out from the 1" foam (Arm Section L). Stick this to the

front of the arm and its edges will be covered by wadding and calico. Slash the surplus calico at the front of the arm cover and stick down on to the foam as seen in Diagram 83.

28. Using the template, cut wadding to fit over the front of the arm and stick in position.

29. Cut a similar shape in calico but allow $\frac{1}{2}''$ turnings. Turn in $\frac{1}{2}''$ and anchor with pins to the arm covering. Secure with blind stitching to the inside and top of the arm. Tack the outside edge to the outside of the arm frame.

30. Cut arm covering fabric as for the calico, but add a fly at the lower edge if necessary. See paragraph Outer Cover, page 122 above. This final cover should only extend $1''$ beyond the front of the arm. (See Diagram 84.) Tack the lower and upper edges in position as for the calico cover.

31. Slash the cover at the back just above the level of the arm. Use the same method of folding back the material as in Diagrams 80 and 81. Take the lower section through and tack it to the outside back of the frame. Anchor the corresponding flap of the undercover over the cover (Ref. paragraph 26).

32. Continue to work the upper section round the arm, slashing if necessary.

33. Tack a layer of wadding and calico to the outside arm. These will give strength under the cover.

34. Cut the outside arm material and attach with 'back tacking' (Diagrams 84 and 91). This material should extend $1''$ beyond the front edge of the arm. Tack the back edge of the material to the outside back of the chair, and the lower edge to the underside of the frame.

35. Snip the $1''$ at the front of the arm cover and with herringbone stitch anchor it to the undercover (Diagram 85).

36. Prepare piping cord to neaten the front arm panels. Pin in position (Diagram 86). Using a circular-needle

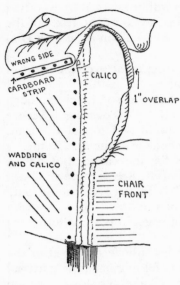

Diagram 84

Diagram 85. Herring-bone stitch secures edges of inside and outside arm to calico undercover

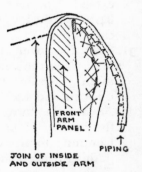

Diagram 86

anchor it with Back Stitch. The stitches will pass between the cord and the machine tacking.

37. Cut the front arm panels allowing ½" turnings. Turn in this allowance, slashing where necessary. Pin in position and secure with blind stitching (Diagram 86).

38. Tack a layer of wadding and calico to the outside back of the chair.

39. Cut and attach the back as the front arm panels.

40. Line the under side of the seat.

★ 14 ★

Cushions

(Photographs 14 and 15)

FOAM CAN BE used in various ways for making different types of cushions. It is possible to buy ready moulded cushions in a variety of sizes and shapes, but often it is necessary to be able to make a cushion of certain measurements to fulfil a particular need.

Cushions may be made from single pieces of solid foam as illustrated by the Garden Bed Chair. Two pieces of foam may be joined together, possibly with doming between them, to give a deep reversible cushion for a fire-side chair, arm-chair or settee, or even for a small neck-cushion. Finally, oddments of foam can be cut up to stuff the sectionalized deck-chair cover. It is possible to buy bags of foam chippings from departmental stores to supplement oddments of foam left over from other upholstery.

GARDEN CHAIR

Most delightful garden furniture is on view every summer, attractive to look at and extremely comfortable to use. The cost, however, does deter many people from enjoying these attractive luxuries. If the basic chair is bought and the cushions made at home, it is possible to have the attractive appearance, and the comfort, for a much smaller expenditure.

Materials

Firm density polyether foam, 1″, 1½″, or 2″ (depending on the thickness required) to fit the chair. (Approx. 6′ 3″ × 1′ 10″.)

Iu

$2\frac{1}{8}$ yds. chintz or satinized cotton 48″ wide
$2\frac{1}{8}$ yds. sailcloth 27″ wide or similar strong fabric
$5\frac{3}{4}$ yds. fine nylon cord

Preparation

1. Cut a paper pattern to fit the chair.
2. Mark round the pattern on the foam and cut $\frac{1}{4}$″ outside this line, keeping the sides vertical.   The foam will then be slightly compressed inside the cover.
3. Place the pattern on the wrong side of the chintz—mark round it (this will be the stitching line) and cut out $\frac{1}{2}$″ outside this line (Section A, Diagram 87).
4. Cut a second piece from chintz using the top 18″ only of the pattern and allow extra 1″ on each side.   This extra width allows fulness for this section to slip over the top of the chair (Section B, Diagram 87).
5. Cut Section A in sailcloth allowing $\frac{1}{2}$″ turnings as in paragraph 3—this is the underside of the cushion.
6. Cut out sufficient pieces for the box to go around the cushion—making these strips 1″ wider than the foam: i.e. allowing $\frac{1}{2}$″ turnings.

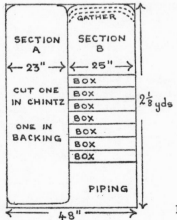

Diagram 87

7. From the remaining chintz prepare cross-way strips $1\frac{1}{4}''$ to $1\frac{1}{2}''$ wide to cover the piping cord. (See sleeve method, Diagrams 5a–d.)

To Assemble the Cover

1. Machine tack the piping into the piping strip (Diagram 6).
2. Join the sections of the box together and draw the stitching lines $\frac{1}{2}''$ from each long edge. Machine on these lines. This extra care will ensure an even box after the cushion has been assembled. The machining will act as a barrier where the box has to be slashed at the corners.
3. Pin and tack the piping round the top of the cushion cover, fitting it to the right side of the fabric. Slash the piping covering at the corners. The pins should be put in on the stitching line of the cover and pass between the machine tacking and the cord. Tack into position. Join the ends as Diagrams 7a and b.
4. Pin the box to the piped edge of the cushion, slashing to the stitched line on the box at the corners. (See Diagram 88.) Tack and machine, using a zipper or piping foot.

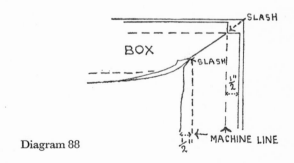

Diagram 88

5. Turn up a $\frac{1}{2}''$ hem along the lower edge of Section B.
6. Run gathering threads $\frac{1}{4}''$ and $\frac{1}{2}''$ from the top of this section and draw up until it fits the back of the cushion.
7. Place the wrong side of the above Section B to the right side of the back of the cushion—tack together and use as one piece of material.
8. Fit this back section to the box—leaving open the lower end. Machine.
9. Fit zipp fastener or Velcro to allow for easy closing of the opening.
   When inserting the rubber cushion, fold it and slide it into the cover. Work the cover over the cushion so that the edges of the box are exactly over the edges of the cushion.

LOOSE REVERSIBLE CUSHION

If a single sheet of cavity foam is used to make a cushion, this cushion will not be reversible. If, in fact, a reversible cushion is required and cavity foam is being used, two pieces must be joined with cavity sides together. Moreover, if a domed cushion is to be made, again two pieces of foam—whatever type is being used—must be joined together with the doming inserted between them.

$\frac{1}{2}''$ or $1''$ solid foam is used for the doming and this is cut $2''$ to $3''$ smaller all round than the top and bottom sections. The three layers are joined together by a thin layer of rubber adhesive. It is very important that the doming is placed exactly in the centre of the cushion.

If cavity foam is being used the top and bottom are cut $\frac{1}{2}''$ smaller all round than the dimension of the final cushion. After they have been joined together, the edges of the cushion are reinforced by strips of $\frac{1}{2}''$ solid foam which form the walls of the cushion.

N.B.: When cutting the walling, two pieces are cut the same length as the wall they are to fit. The other two pieces are each 1″ longer than the other two sides of the cavity as illustrated in the example below.

OBLONG CUSHION FROM 2″ *CAVITY FOAM* (*final size* 20″ × 24″)

2 pieces 2″ cavity 19″ × 23″
1 piece 1″ solid 13″ × 17″—doming
2 pieces ½″ solid 4″ × 23″ ⎫
2 pieces ½″ solid 4″ × 20″ ⎬ walling

SHAPED HEAD CUSHION

Materials
2 pieces 1½″ foam 16″ × 8″
2 pieces calico 18″ × 2″ ⎫
2 pieces calico 9″ × 2″ ⎬ walling

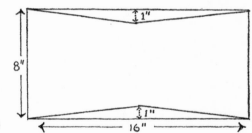

Diagram 89

Method
1. Cut paper pattern to the above shape.
2. Mark pattern on both pieces of foam and cut out.
3. Feather both pieces of foam to within ½″ from the top side of the foam (Diagrams 14a and 14d).
4. Place a thin layer of adhesive round the unfeathered ½″ of each half of the cushion.
5. Allow adhesive to go tacky and join the two sections together.   Stick calico over the joins.

133

Cover

Materials

¼ yd. 48" material

1½ yds. nylon cord.

1. Cut the two sections of the cover ⅜" larger all round than the template. By taking ½" turnings the cover will be slightly smaller than the cushion and so it will not wrinkle or move in use.
2. Cover the cord with crossway strips. Baste the piping to the right side of one section of the cover.
3. Fit the two sides of the cover together with the right sides inside.
4. Machine, leaving open 1 short side, and insert a zipp at this end.
5. Insert the rubber pad.

DECK CHAIR CUSHION

This most useful cushion can be stuffed with the oddments of foam left over from other upholstery. These are cut into pieces the size of a walnut. If extra foam is needed bags of 'chippings' are available in many shops.

Materials

1¾ yds. furnishing fabric 48" wide

Sufficient foam for stuffing

Method

1. From the furnishing fabric cut
   2 strips 59" × 19" for the cushion (58" × 18" finished)
   2 strips 9" × 6" for straps.
2. Turn in ½" all round both the large oblongs. Mitre the corners (Diagrams 21a and b). Fit and pin these with wrong sides together.
3. Fold the long edge of each strap to the centre so that the raw edges run down the middle. Fold again to give 2 straps 9" × 1½". Machine down each long edge (Diagram 90).

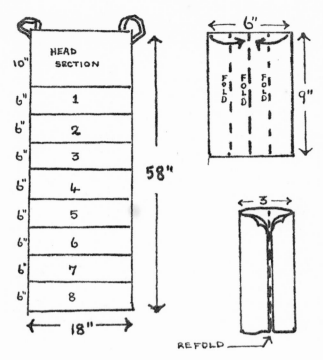

Diagram 90. *Left:* Finished cushion

Above: strap open
Below: strap folded once

4. Fit these straps between the two halves of the cushion as shown. Test to ensure that the loops fit tightly over the rounded ends of the chair.
5. Machine along the bottom edge, one long edge, the top edge and down 4″ of head section of the other long edge.
6. Mark the horizontal lines at distances as shown in Diagram 90. Machine on these lines to form the pockets. Fill the pockets. Tack the second long side and machine.

⋆ 15 ⋆

A Box Ottoman

THIS METHOD CAN be used for renovating a box which has been previously upholstered. It may also be used to convert an old wooden box into a useful and attractive piece of household furniture. An ottoman is particularly useful in a bedroom or bathroom and can be covered with material which matches the other furnishings in the room. Smaller boxes make excellent containers for slippers, toys and magazines. If they are sufficiently strong they can also be used as an additional seat.

If the box has been previously upholstered it must be stripped of the old upholstery, and all the tacks removed. When an old box is being used, it should be thoroughly cleaned and all the edges rubbed down with glass paper to avoid cutting the covering material. The lid must be removed and the hinges cleaned if necessary.

Upholstering the Lid

This is upholstered in exactly the same way as the Contemporary Stool. If the box is larger than $12'' \times 18''$, the finished lid will have an improved appearance if $\frac{1}{2}''$ or $1''$ doming is used, as with large stools. (See Diagram 32b.) If the lid is to close properly the lining must fit inside the thickness of the wood—hence the tacks holding the cover in position must be inserted well away from the edge of the lid. The lining should be chosen to tone with the covering fabric.

Covering the Box

1. Cut a piece of wadding or $\frac{1}{8}''$ polyether foam to fit each of the four outer sides of the box, and stick these into

position. This gives a padded appearance to the covered box.

2. To prepare the outer cover, cut a strip of material for each side. Allow 1″ turnings on all the edges. If the wood of the box is $\frac{1}{2}$″ thick or more, allow 1$\frac{1}{2}$″ turnings at the top of each strip. The selvedge must run vertically down the cover, and if the material is patterned the front of the box must match the lid. With small boxes it may be possible to cut the front and two side sections in one piece. A separate piece is then cut for the back.

3. Baste the sections securely together into one long strip and fit around the box. The seams must come exactly on the corners of the box.

4. Machine the join(s) leaving 1″ or 1$\frac{1}{2}$″ unstitched (depending on the thickness of the wood—see paragraph 2) at the top and the bottom of each seam. Trim the seams to $\frac{1}{2}$″.

5. Fit the cover around the box so that 1″ of the cover extends above and below the sides and so that the final join will fall on one back corner. Anchor with temporary tacks.

6. At the back corner, turn in the surplus material at each end of the cover and trim to $\frac{1}{2}$″. Pin these edges together. By using a circular needle and blind stitching (see Diagram 50) the seam will be invisibly closed.

7. At the bottom, turn the surplus inch of material under the box, and mitre the corners. Tack into position.

8. At the top edge, again mitre the material at the corners, and take the surplus material to the inside of the box and tack into position, keeping the tacks close to the edge of the fabric. If the covering fabric is thick it may be necessary to cut away the fabric where the hinges are to be fixed.

Cutting and Fitting the Lining

Again the inside of the box may be lined with wadding or foam, but this is optional. This padding should extend from the bottom of the box to the edge of the covering fabric.

9. Cut a section of lining for each side allowing ½″ turnings at the sides, 1″ at the top, and 2″ at the bottom.

10. Baste together, fit in the box, and machine, leaving the bottom 2″ of the seams unstitched. Neaten the lower edge.

11. Cut strips of cardboard ½″ wide, one for each side of the box.

12. Place the top edge of the lining to the edge of the covering material—the right side of the lining to the box, and the main lining held above the box. (See Diagram 91.)

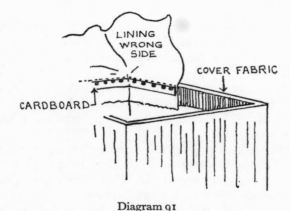

Diagram 91

13. Tack one cardboard strip along each edge of the box— the top of the cardboard to be approximately ⅛″ below the top of the box. The tacks must be along the extreme top edge of the cardboard so that it will not bend when the lining is folded back over it. The heads of the tacks must not extend over the card or they will cut the lining. The lining is then folded over the cardboard and a smooth sharp edge will result. This process is known as back tacking. If the cardboard is omitted

the lining will have a scalloped edge, looping down between the tacks. Stick the surplus 2″ at the lower edge of the lining to the bottom of the box.

Neatening the Bottom

14. Cut a piece of hardboard to fit into the box with $\frac{1}{4}″$ clearance all round. Pad this with $\frac{1}{8}″$ polyether foam or wadding.
15. Cover the padding with a piece of the lining material, taking it over to the underside of the board and sticking down the edges. Drop this into the box.

Adding Feet

16. Neaten the underside of the ottoman with hessian. Either four domed feet or small castors may be fitted.

⋆ 16 ⋆

Bed Heads

(Photographs 15 and 16)

PADDED BED HEADS are becoming very fashionable again. They can be divided mainly into two groups. There are those which have deep buttoning and are usually covered with a soft woven fabric, such as velvet, textured silks, or satinized cottons. Then there are those with a shallow type buttoning commonly used with vinyl coverings.

Modern fabrics and modern dry cleaning agents have overcome the argument that padded headboards are unpractical and unhygienic. The modern vinyl-type fabrics can be sponged. Aerosol type cleaners which can be used on most upholstery fabrics are now on the market. After using these cleaners, careful brushing will keep these rather exotic looking furnishings immaculate and attractive.

In choosing covering fabric, problems can arise with headboards which are more than three feet in width. For larger headboards it is desirable to avoid joins in the cover. If possible choose a fabric which can be used with the selvedge running parallel to the lower edge of the board. This will eliminate the use of prints which have a floral pattern running down them. Although contrary to the usual rules of furnishing, even velvet can be used satisfactorily with the pile running horizontally, if this is the fabric a worker wishes to use. It must be remembered that the result will be slightly different in colour to that obtained when the pile runs downwards as when making curtains.

140

Buttons

When using soft fabrics, covering buttons presents no problems. There are on the market button moulds in a range of sizes, and cutting templates are found on the card to which these moulds are attached. The $\frac{1}{2}''$ and $\frac{3}{4}''$ buttons give a well balanced effect for deep buttoning. Some covering materials allow the reflection of the metal to shine through a single layer. To prevent this a second circle of fabric, the exact size of the top of the button is stuck to the metal mould with a thin layer of adhesive. If double material is used for the whole button cover, difficulty may be experienced when fixing the under part of the button. If the material is rather bulky, press the parts of the button together over a cotton bobbin. The shank will fit into the central hole of the bobbin.

When using vinyl or leather it may be necessary to shave off some of the back of the material to make covering possible. Alternatively, some commercial upholsterers will provide this service for the home worker. A larger mould can be used with these fabrics.

Headboards

The upholstery can be worked most easily on solid wood. If an old polished headboard exists this can be used, but it will never be able to be used unpadded again as holes will be bored into it. However, as the wooden base can be the most expensive item it may be more practical to use one already possessed unless it is a valuable antique. Alternatively, a bedhead can be cut in $\frac{1}{2}''$ ply-wood or $\frac{3}{4}''$ block-board.

The design of the board should be very simple. If a shaped board is chosen, the outline should flow smoothly. Small curves and deep indentations should be avoided when deep buttoning is to be worked as both cause difficulty when drawing materials over the back of the board.

Foam

Polyether foam is extremely suitable for use on head-boards. For deep buttoning 3″ foam gives a result very luxurious in appearance. For shallow buttoning, 1″ or 2″ foam gives a more satisfactory result. Some headboards are completely upholstered (Style A, Diagram 93)—others have the lower 4″ to 6″ left without padding, depending on the depth of the mattress. The unpadded board fits behind the mattress and is covered with wadding and covering fabric after the buttoning has been completed. This is described as style B (Diagram 93).

Requirements

Single 3 ft. beds:
1 headboard
Polyether foam 1″ to 1½″ all round larger than the part of the board to be upholstered
1½ yds. calico 36″ wide
¾ to 1 yd. covering fabric 48″ wide—depending on the height of the board
1½ yds. lining sateen for the back of the bedhead
Brace and ⅛″ or 3⁄16″ bit
Upholstery twine
Button moulds
⅜″ fine tacks
Adhesive

Double 4′ 6″ beds:

As above except
2 yds. calico 48″ wide
2 yds. covering fabric 48″ wide

Positioning the Buttons

The most usual designs employed are those based on the diamond. The shape and size of the diamond can be varied according to the choice of the worker, the nature of the covering fabric and the size of the headboard (Diagram 92).

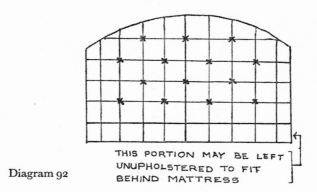

THIS PORTION MAY BE LEFT
UNUPHOLSTERED TO FIT
BEHIND MATTRESS

Diagram 92

The rows of buttons can vary from 4″ to 6″ apart and the buttons from 8″ to 10″, but even these measurements are not to be regarded as rigid. It is very important that the buttons should be kept well away from the edge of the board—a minimum of 3″ or 4″. If buttons are too close to the edge of the board the final edge will have an uneven outline. The aim must be to have the edges quite smooth in contour. The position of the buttons must always be marked, and the headboard then erected behind the bed, and the effect studied.

The holes should be bored with a $\frac{1}{8}$″ or $\frac{3}{16}$″ bit—and should be sufficiently large to allow the mattress needle to pass through easily when threaded with twine.

Preparing the Foam

1. Place the board on the foam, leaving 1″ to $1\frac{1}{2}$″ border all round the edge. If the lower 4″ to 6″ is to be left unupholstered, reduce the normal depth of the foam by this amount: i.e. 1″ to $1\frac{1}{2}$″ will be allowed at the top

143

edge and 1″ to 1½″ below the final upholstery line. (See Diagrams 93 A and B.)

2. Draw the cutting line 1″ to 1½″ outside the edge of the board and cut—keeping the edges as vertical as possible. Do not feather the edge as a very rounded finish is required.

3. Tear strips of calico 4″ to 5″ deep and iron. Attach to the foam in the order shown in Diagram 94.

STYLE A

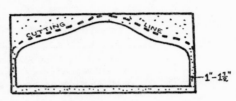

STYLE B

Diagram 93

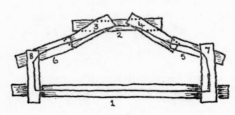

Diagram 94

Attaching the Foam

Method A.   If the board is to be completely upholstered.

4. Place the foam on to a table calicoed side downwards, and place the board on top of it.

5a. Turn in the extra foam under the board, bring the calico up and on to the back of the board and place in temporary tacks about every 6″ along top and bottom edges.

6a. Complete the final tacking of lower edge—keeping the calico very tight.

7a. Complete tacking of top edge and then the side edges as for the Contemporary Stool.   Make sure that the foam comes absolutely to the edge of the wood and that it cannot be pushed back on the curves; i.e. the calico MUST be pulled very tightly.   Trim off all surplus calico.

Method B

Work as for Method A to No. 5

5b. Temporary tack top and side edges.
    Turn the board with foam uppermost and temporary tack calico to upholstery line 4″ to 6″ from lower edge of the board.

6b. Tack lower edge with tacks placed through the calico at the edge of the foam and hammer into the upholstery line.   This method is similar to that used for pincushion seats but here the foam is not feathered.   (See Diagram 34).   7b as 7a.

Buttoning Method A

With most fabric covers, other than thicker ones, such as velvet, it is advisable to attach an undercover of calico. This is not necessary when using plastic coated fabrics for the cover.   The same method is used for attaching the undercover as the final cover.   Equal care must be taken with the disposal of fulness and the placing of the pleats.

Those of the undercover must be exactly under those of the top cover. If an undercover is used the top cover may easily be replaced if a new scheme of furnishing is required. To enable the buttons to be successfully removed without disturbing the buttoning of the undercover, a standard procedure of buttoning is recommended. See following paragraphs Nos. 9 and 16.

N.B. It is of the greatest importance that sufficient margin of fabric is allowed all round the board for deep buttoning. The material is drawn in as the buttons are attached and pulled tightly into position. A minimum of nine inches should be left around a headboard for a 4' 6" bed, but this varies depending on the number of buttons used. Always commence buttoning from the central hole and work outwards from this button.

8. Place the undercover on the table with the headboard over it—with the foam to the calico. Temporary tack the calico loosely to the back of the board. This makes for ease of working. Care must be taken to keep the grain of the material running horizontally across the headboard.

9. With the board uppermost place two $\frac{3}{8}''$ fine tacks on the horizontal line through the central hole: one on

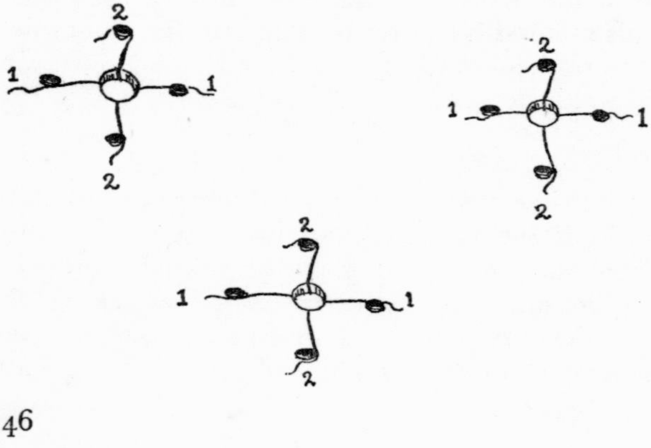

Diagram 95

either side of the hole. Do not hammer them down but leave sufficient space for the twine to be wound around them (Diagram 95—Tacks No. 1).

10. Thread the needle with twine and secure one end of the thread under one tack. Hammer this tack firmly into position.

11. Take the needle through the board and foam, and unthread the needle.

12. From the back of the board re-insert the eye-end of the needle and push the needle through the foam until the eye emerges on the front of the foam. Angle the entry of the needle so that the point emerges not less than $\frac{1}{2}''$ from the twine. Rethread the needle and draw it back through the board.

13. Draw up the thread and wind it around the second tack. When the thread is sufficiently tight, hammer in the second tack.

14. Turn board with the foam uppermost. Smooth the material away from the button position and press the finger firmly into the foam where the next button is to be placed. Arrange the fulness in a diagonal pleat. This should face downwards to avoid collecting dust (Diagram 96). Continue the buttoning, working diagonally away from the centre. It is important to test each button position before finally securing it to avoid 'waisting' or excess fulness between the buttons.

Finishing the Edge (Diagram 96)

15. The surplus fabric on the edges is disposed of by horizontal or vertical pleats on the straight edges. On curved edges the pleats may run diagonally from the button position, but the two sides of a headboard must be symmetrical. Vertical pleats on the top and bottom edges may be inverted pleats or single pleats facing the centre of the board. The surplus material is tacked to the back of the board about $\frac{1}{2}''$ from the edge.

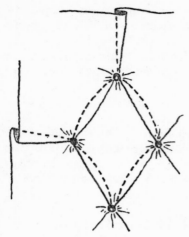

Diagram 96

Style B

This is worked in exactly the same way, up to the finishing of the lower edge. This is tacked to the upholstery line, the fulness as in Style A being arranged in vertical pleats.

The Cover. Styles A & B

16a. This is attached for either style in the same way as the undercover with two modifications:

    (i) when fixing the two tacks to which the twine is secured they are placed above and below the hole. (Diagram 95—Tacks No. 2.) It is these tacks only which are removed when a new cover is to be fitted or if a button needs adjusting.

    (ii) The button is threaded on to the twine before the needle is rethreaded as in paragraph 12.

Neatening the Unpadded Board—Style B

16b. Trim the lower edges of both the underlining and the cover to 1″. Stick a layer of wadding to the unupholstered board. Cut a strip of the cover material 7″–9″

deep depending on the depth of the mattress (4″–6″) and attach this by 'back tacking' (see Diagrams 84 and 91) to cover the raw edges of the covers of the upholstered board. Bring this strip over the wadding and tack it to the back of the board.

Neatening the back of the board

17a and b. Trim away any surplus materials to within $\frac{1}{2}$″ of the tacks.

18a and b. Cut a piece of wadding $\frac{1}{2}$″ less all round than the board and stick this to the board.

19a and b. Cut the back lining $\frac{3}{8}$″ larger than the board. Turn in $\frac{1}{2}$″ slashing where necessary to produce a flat turning.

20a and b. Pin into position and secure with blind-stitching (Diagram 50).

PANELLED HEAD BOARD

The headboard in Photograph 15 has a removable central panel. This panel was upholstered as a drop-in seat (Chapter 6) using 1″ polyether foam and then screwed back into position.

The National Rubber Producers Research Association, 19 Buckingham Street, Adelphi, London W.C.2.

The Russell Trading Company Limited, 13 Norton Street, London Road, Liverpool 3, for Chair Frames, Stool Parts, Boxes and Ottomans.

Distinctive Trimmings Co. Ltd., 17d Kensington Church Street, London W.8., for Braids, Gimps and Cords.

Index